LIVING
the covenant

Participant Guide

Episodes 9–16

Abingdon Press

COVENANT BIBLE STUDY
LIVING THE COVENANT: PARTICIPANT GUIDE

This book is printed on acid-free paper.

ISBN 978-1-4267-7217-7

Printed in the United States of America

15 16 17 18 19 20 21 22 23—10 9 8 7 6 5 4 3 2

Covenant Bible Study resources include:

Creating the Covenant: Participant Guide, ISBN 978-1-4267-7216-0 (large print ISBN 978-1-63088-625-7)
Living the Covenant: Participant Guide, ISBN 978-1-4267-7217-7 (large print ISBN 978-1-63088-626-4)
Trusting the Covenant: Participant Guide, ISBN 978-1-4267-7218-4 (large print ISBN 978-1-63088-627-1)
Covenant Bible Study App: Participant Guides for iOS and Android, ISBN 978-1-4267-7219-1

Covenant Bible Study: Covenant Meditations, ISBN 978-1-4267-7220-7
Covenant Bible Study: Covenant Meditations ePub, ISBN 978-1-4267-7221-4
Covenant Bible Study App: Covenant Meditations for iOS and Android, ISBN 978-1-4267-7222-1

Covenant Bible Study: Leader Guide, ISBN 978-1-4267-7223-8
Covenant Bible Study: Leader Guide ePub, ISBN 978-1-4267-7225-2
Covenant Bible Study App: Leader Guide for iOS and Android, ISBN 978-1-4267-7224-5

Covenant Bible Study: DVD Video (set of three), ISBN 978-1-4267-8678-5
Covenant Bible Study: MP4 Video Episodes (download individually from CovenantBibleStudy.com)

CEB Study Bible, hardcover ISBN 978-1-6092-6028-6, decotone ISBN 978-1-6092-6040-8
CEB Study Bible: Large Print Edition, hardcover ISBN 978-1-60926-176-4

To order resources or to obtain additional information for participants, Covenant groups, and leaders, go to www.CovenantBibleStudy.com or to www.cokesbury.com. All print resources are available exclusively from these online sites, from Cokesbury reps, or by calling Cokesbury (800-672-1789). The Covenant Bible Study digital app is available from iTunes and Google Play.

LIVING
the covenant

Contents

LIVING
the covenant

Covenant Group Participants and Leader

Name	Phone	E-mail

Covenant Group Meeting Location _____

Covenant Group Meeting Day and Time _____

CovenantBibleStudy.com username _____ password _____

Bible Readings at a Glance

Sign up with your group at CovenantBibleStudy.com to get daily readings by e-mail from your group leader.

Episode 9

Day 1	Ruth 1–2	Famine, loss, and exile	❑
Day 2	Ruth 3–4	Redemption and restoration	❑
Day 3	Esther 1–4	Plot	❑
Day 4	Esther 5–8	Counterplot	❑
Day 5	Song of Songs 1–2; 4:1-7; 5:10-16	Love unplugged	❑
Day 6	Covenant Meditation on Song of Songs 8:6-7*a*	God loves you.	❑
Day 7	Group Meeting Experience with Ruth 1:8-18	Solemn promise for life	❑

Episode 10

Day 1	Luke 1:1–4:30	Jesus fulfills hopes and confounds expectations.	❑
Day 2	Luke 10:25-37; 13; 15; 16:19–17:19; 18:1-17; 19:1-10	Jesus proclaims God's kingdom.	❑
Day 3	Luke 22–24	Jesus, the rejected prophet, dies and rises again.	❑
Day 4	Acts 1–4	Jesus' followers receive power from the Holy Spirit.	❑
Day 5	Acts 8:1*b*–11:18	Unlikely newcomers join the church.	❑
Day 6	Covenant Meditation on Acts 2:42-47	Teaching, prayers, and shared meals	❑
Day 7	Group Meeting Experience with Luke 4:14-30	Jesus preaches in his synagogue.	❑

Episode 11

❏	Day 1	2 Samuel 7; 9; 11–12	David's use and abuse of power
❏	Day 2	1 Kings 11–13	Loss of Israel
❏	Day 3	1 Kings 17–19; 21	King versus prophet
❏	Day 4	2 Kings 17–19	The fall of Samaria and the northern kingdom
❏	Day 5	2 Kings 22–25	The fall of Jerusalem and the southern kingdom
❏	Day 6	Covenant Meditation on 2 Kings 5:1-14	Who is the leader?
❏	Day 7	Group Meeting Experience with 2 Samuel 7:1-17	Covenant with David

Episode 12

❏	Day 1	1 Thessalonians 1–5	Encouragement for faithful living
❏	Day 2	2 Thessalonians 1–3	Harassed
❏	Day 3	1 Timothy 1:1-2; 2–4; 6:1-2, 11-15	Discernment
❏	Day 4	2 Timothy 1–4	An ethical will
❏	Day 5	Titus	Baptism and the Holy Spirit fuel faithful living.
❏	Day 6	Covenant Meditation on 2 Timothy 3:14-17	Scripture is useful.
❏	Day 7	Group Meeting Experience with 1 Thessalonians 1:2-10	Thanksgiving

Episode 13

❏	Day 1	Proverbs 1–4	Learning discernment
❏	Day 2	Proverbs 10–15	Speaking the truth
❏	Day 3	Proverbs 25–29	Using power and influence wisely
❏	Day 4	Ecclesiastes 1–4	When life seems pointless
❏	Day 5	Ecclesiastes 9–12	Everyday moments of joy
❏	Day 6	Covenant Meditation on Ecclesiastes 3:1-8	What is good for my life?
❏	Day 7	Group Meeting Experience with Proverbs 2:1-19	How to become wise

Episode 14

Day 1	Philemon	Reconciliation of "brothers"	❏
Day 2	Philippians 1–4	Reconciliation and the fellowship of believers	❏
Day 3	Colossians 1:1–3:17	Reconciliation as the hidden treasure of God	❏
Day 4	Ephesians 1:1–5:20	Reconciliation as the cosmic reality	❏
Day 5	Colossians 3:18–4:1; Ephesians 5:21–6:9	A reconciled household	❏
Day 6	Covenant Meditation on Philemon 1:4-7	Reconciled in Christ	❏
Day 7	Group Meeting Experience with Ephesians 2	From death to reconciled life	❏

Episode 15

Day 1	James 1–2	Faith and impartiality	❏
Day 2	James 3–5	Penitence and patience	❏
Day 3	1 Peter 1:3–4:11	New life guided by Christ	❏
Day 4	1 Peter 4:12–5:14	Waiting for the last days	❏
Day 5	Jude and 2 Peter	When the great day is delayed	❏
Day 6	Covenant Meditation on James 1:22-26	Doers of the word	❏
Day 7	Group Meeting Experience with 1 Peter 2:4-10	Chosen people	❏

Episode 16

Day 1	Isaiah 1; 5:1–7:17; 9:2-7; 11:1-10	Royal prophet	❏
Day 2	Hosea 1:1-9; 2; 11:1-9	How can I give you up, Ephraim?	❏
Day 3	Amos 1:1–3:8; 5; 7:10-17	A lion has roared.	❏
Day 4	Micah 1:1–3:12; 6:1-8	What the Lord requires from you	❏
Day 5	Zephaniah 1; 3; Malachi 3–4	The great day of the Lord is near.	❏
Day 6	Covenant Meditation on Micah 6:8	Justice, love, and humility	❏
Day 7	Group Meeting Experience with Amos 5:7-24	Seek good.	❏

LIVING
the covenant

Covenant Creative Team

Editorial

Theodore Hiebert, Old Testament Editor

Jaime Clark-Soles, New Testament Editor

Magrey deVega, Leadership Editor

Pam Hawkins, Meditations Editor

David Teel, Project Manager

Paul Franklyn, General Editor and Associate Publisher

Neil M. Alexander, Publisher

Video Cohosts

Christine Chakoian, Senior Pastor,
    First Presbyterian Church, Lake Forest, IL

Shane Stanford, Senior Pastor,
    Christ United Methodist Church, Memphis, TN

Writers: Living the Covenant

Episode 9   Judy Fentress-Williams, Professor of Old Testament, Virginia Theological Seminary, Alexandria, VA

Episode 10   Matthew L. Skinner, Associate Professor of New Testament, Luther Seminary, St. Paul, MN

Episode 11   Roy L. Heller, Associate Professor of Old Testament, Perkins School of Theology, Dallas, TX

Episode 12   Audrey L. S. West, Adjunct Professor of New Testament, Lutheran School of Theology, Chicago, IL

Episode 13   Christine Roy Yoder, Professor of Old Testament Language, Literature, and Exegesis, Columbia Theological Seminary, Decatur, GA

Episode 14   Michael J. Brown, Academic Dean, Payne Theological Seminary, Wilberforce, OH

Episode 15   David L. Bartlett, Professor Emeritus of Christian Communication, Yale Divinity School, New Haven, CT

Episode 16   Francisco García-Treto, Jennie Farris Railey King Professor Emeritus of Religion, Trinity University, San Antonio, TX

Production and Design

Christy Lynch, Production Editor

Jeff Moore, Packaging and Interior Design

Emily Keafer Lambright, Interior Design

PerfecType, Typesetting

Robert Dupuy, Covenant App Developer

CovenantBibleStudy.com

Christie Durand, Analyst

Gregory Davis, Developer

David Burns, Designer

Dan Heile, Database Analyst

Video Production: Revolution Pictures, Inc.

Randy Brewer, Executive Producer

Michelle Abnet, Producer

Ry Cox, Codirector

Jeff Venable, Codirector

Chris Adams, Photography Director

Brandon Eller, Prop Master

Dave Donnelly, Post Editor

Perry Trest, Colorist

Ruth, Esther, Song of Songs

FAITHFUL LOVE
Committed relationships

Bible Readings

Day 1: Ruth 1–2

Day 2: Ruth 3–4

Day 3: Esther 1–4

Day 4: Esther 5–8

Day 5: Song of Songs 1–2; 4:1-7; 5:10-16

Day 6: Covenant Meditation on Song of Songs 8:6-7a

Day 7: Group Meeting Experience with Ruth 1:8-18

Covenant Prayer

For those who are suffering in the midst of a dysfunctional family

Your faithful love is priceless, God! Humanity finds refuge in the shadow of your wings. (Psalm 36:7)

For those who celebrate their identity in God's family

Heaven thanks you for your wondrous acts, LORD—for your faithfulness too— in the assembly of the holy ones. (Psalm 89:5)

OUR LONGING FOR RELATIONSHIP

A covenant creates a new identity, making a family out of unrelated individuals. A covenant expects faithfulness but also the possibility for love.

9

POSSIBILITY OF LOYAL LOVE

The biblical understanding of the covenant relationship between God and God's people, and among God's people themselves, is shaped and informed by the actual covenants, or agreements, common in Israel's social life. The books of Ruth, Esther, and the Song of Songs explore the committed relationships that are the basis of a covenant.

Sometimes we wonder why these books (especially Song of Songs) were included in the scriptures. But they are an important part of the canon because they use marriage as an analogy for God's covenant love. The marriage covenant creates a new identity, making a family out of unrelated individuals, and unlike economic or political contracts, a marriage covenant expects faithfulness but also allows the possibility for love. Some think a covenant is a contract. A contract, however, is usually a last resort, invoked after a relationship has already failed and is unlikely to recover.

By exploring these stories of marriage relationships and the loyalty and love within them, we can learn more about the nature of covenant relationships in the Bible. We can also learn more about the relationship of women and men in biblical society. While biblical society was patriarchal, investing men with primary prestige and power, these are stories of strong women who work in and around male structures with strength, dignity, and integrity. For Ruth and Esther, their futures and the futures of their people lay in their hands.

RUTH

Ruth is a beautifully written story of loss and recovery, famine and harvest, death and new life. The family of Elimelech and Naomi experiences a series of tragedies. Naomi loses the things that define her and faces an uncertain future. The family's very survival is in jeopardy. As a woman and an outsider, Ruth is the unlikely heroine. Her faithfulness to the covenant she made with her husband and with Naomi's family enables the family to survive.

The narrative of this family's destruction and reconstruction can be dated to the time of the exile, the time of Israel's national destruction. The exiled people of Israel were worried about survival and identity. In the narrative of Ruth, they heard a story of a foreign woman who ensures the family's survival and allows for a renewed identity. The story invites its hearers to consider whether God's covenant relationship is for Israel and Israel alone.

ESTHER

The book of Esther takes place in the Persian court. It was written when the people of Israel were no longer in their homeland. The events in the narrative take place during the fourth or third century BCE, the time of the Jewish diaspora, when Jews had been dispersed throughout the countries of the Mediterranean world. Many of the practices unique to Judaism were lost over the years as later generations of Jews took on names and practices that reflected the languages and cultures of their conquerors. In this new situation, assimilation was necessary for survival. Once assimilation became a way of life, the community had to determine what the core elements of Jewish identity were when their nation, king, temple, and priesthood were long gone. What were the terms of the covenant in Persia? Would God be faithful?

> **Optional:** *An additional video on Ruth and Esther is available for download from* **CovenantBibleStudy.com**.

Esther can be described as a court tale, a narrative that portrays Jews living under foreign rule and subject to the laws of a king who doesn't know their God. In the majority of these stories, a crisis arises when the rules of the king stand in opposition to the covenant practices or God-given commands that are unique to Jewish identity as God's chosen people. In Esther, the reader is introduced to a community whose lives are in danger. The community is threatened not only with the loss of life but with the loss of identity, essential to survival. Esther finds herself in a place of privilege and must decide if she will identify with her people and thereby expose herself to the dangers they face as a community under foreign rule.

SONG OF SONGS

The Song of Songs, also known as the Song of Solomon, is a collection of love poems that has long intrigued and confused its readers. Written in the late fourth or third century BCE, the expressions of affection and desire between the two lovers form a dialogue, or a call and response between the woman and the man. The poetry is sensual. It appeals to the senses of taste, touch, smell, sound, and sight, describing a human love that is without restraint. The sensuality of the poetry and the imagery of the garden evoke Eden's garden, with two people in a sanctuary where all their needs are met. However, as the poetry reveals, the lovers aren't always together. When they aren't together, the energy of the poetry is focused on being together. The lovers fill the space that separates them with language, imagining the dearly loved partner, making promises for the next meeting, or simply expressing the all-consuming desire to be reunited.

Both the woman and the man use symbolic language to praise the dearly loved partner and to convey the urgency of longing and desire. Metaphor and simile are used in analogies. The lovers use the language of familiar things to describe the indescribable. This symbolic language invites us to enter the garden of delights and experience agony with the lovers. Like the speakers, we know the experience of closeness and separation in our own relationships.

And like Israel, we also know what it is to be intimate with and alienated from God. Over the years, interpreters have taken the real and intense human love reflected in this poetry as symbolic of the love between God and God's people. The dialogue of the poetry invites us to embrace the dynamic of longing that comes from being apart and the joy that comes from being united because it sheds light on our relationship with the creator.

The Festival Scroll—Purim, Weeks, and Passover: In the Hebrew text of the Bible, Ruth, Esther, and the Song of Songs are grouped together within the festival scroll known in Hebrew as the *Megilloth*. These three narratives are associated with specific festivals that are a part of the Jewish calendar. Esther is associated with the celebration of Purim. The celebration of this holiday includes the reading and retelling of Esther's story. Ruth is associated with the Festival of Weeks (Hebrew *Shavuot*), a harvest celebration, and the Song of Songs is read during Passover. These three books continue to be part of the ongoing life in communities of faith. They demonstrate that the covenant is more than a contract. Rather, these books vividly present in story and song the responsibilities and privileges of a committed relationship.

Ruth, Esther, and Song of Songs are grouped together in the Megilloth, or festival scroll. Ruth's story is retold during the Festival of Weeks (a harvest celebration commemorating the gift of Torah instruction at Sinai). Esther's story is told during Purim (celebrating deliverance from Haman's plot to kill the Jewish people in the Persian Empire). Song of Songs is recited during Passover, celebrating the rescue and liberation of the Hebrew people from slavery in Egypt.

Day 1: Ruth 1–2

Famine, loss, and exile

The book of Ruth is a beautifully constructed narrative with shifts in location and plot twists that create a crisis for the family of Elimelech and Naomi. These elements are also signs of comedy. In the story of Ruth these elements are used to explore the theme of identity. The characters in the story are subject to loss of identity through famine, migration, and death. For them (and us), key markers of identity are name, homeland, and people (including family, tribe, and nationality). In Ruth 1, the family moves away from their homeland, the men die, and—since lineage and descent are reckoned through males—the name or identity of this family is facing certain extinction.

The names of the characters provide clues to the reader: *Elimelech* means "my God is king." His wife's name, *Naomi*, means "full and/or pleasant." The names of the sons are *Mahlon* and *Chilion*, meaning "sickly" and "destruction," or "frail," respectively. *Orpah* means "back of the neck," and *Ruth* means "to saturate" or "to water." As you read, consider the extent to which the characters live up to their names or reputations.

> **Optional:** *An additional video retelling the story of Ruth is available for download from* **CovenantBibleStudy.com**.

Ruth's ethnicity as a Moabite is important. Though this story doesn't speak disrespectfully of the Moabites, they were despised by some Israelite writers. When the text describes Ruth as a Moabite, it is identifying her as a person who some would have considered an outsider of the worst kind. Early hearers of this story would have had contempt for the Moabites. Ruth's story forces us to think about how God may work through those we designate as "outsiders," "opponents," or "enemies."

What type of person would you (or the people in your zip code) think of as an outsider?

Day 2: Ruth 3–4
Redemption and restoration

The second half of the narrative about Ruth is focused on levirate marriage as a form of redemption. Levirate marriage is a practice that allows for the closest living male relative to "marry" a childless widow. This is for the purposes of providing a male child and ensuring that there is someone to inherit on behalf of the deceased for his surviving family members. It is a useful image of redemption because redemption means to buy back that which was lost. Boaz is the closest male relative who is willing to play the role of redeemer, but in this role he marries Ruth, a Moabite. Ruth's first marriage to an Israelite, Mahlon, occurs under the circumstances of famine, death, and displacement for the Israelite family. Her second marriage takes place during the season of harvest. Boaz is a dutiful redeemer, but he is impressed by Ruth's faithfulness. The term "faithfulness" is often used to describe God's undying commitment to Israel. In this story, a Moabite woman embodies that faithfulness and undying love that God has for God's people.

It shouldn't be lost on the reader that the redemption and restoration of the family involves a plan that takes place under the cover of darkness in Ruth 3, and at the city gate, a public place, during the day in Ruth 4. Similarly, God's work of redemption and restoration can take on a variety of patterns and include unlikely characters. David's genealogy at the conclusion of the book includes a Moabite woman.

How does Ruth's relationship to Israel's dearly loved king change the way Israel feels about the Moabites?

Day 3: Esther 1–4
Plot

This story is a court tale, a literary form used for the narratives in Daniel 1–6 and for the book of Esther. In this story type, the hero or heroine is in the court of a foreign king who is temperamental and easily manipulated by his advisors, who are enemies of the Jewish people. A crisis arises when the advisors convince the king to issue an edict that goes against a covenant practice central to the Jewish faith. In the book of Daniel, the king forces the main characters to take a stand on issues such as dietary teaching and worship practices and to risk their safety in order to abide by the instructions of God's covenant. The story ends with the triumph of the hero (Daniel), and the message to Jews in the diaspora is that God is faithful to the covenant and to God's people who are loyal to the covenant.

Esther is a court tale with a heroine and with a twist. When Esther, or Hadassah (her Hebrew name), becomes queen, she finds herself in a position of privilege, but her identity as a Jew is unknown. We don't have any indication that she is observant of Jewish Instruction and practices. When Haman plots to kill the Jews and a crisis arises, Esther must decide whether or not she will reveal her Jewish identity and risk her life. If she doesn't, she can't save her people (Esth 4:13-14).

The narrative uses elaborate and excessive detail to describe the Persian Empire. By contrast, there is no mention of God. In Esther 4, Mordecai takes on the traditional signs of mourning, and Esther fasts. The turning point in the narrative comes when Esther decides to disclose her Jewish identity and face the king on behalf of her people. Her fate and the fate of her people lie on her shoulders.

Think of a time when you had a choice about disclosing personal information to a group or to another individual. Perhaps it was at school, at work, with friends, or in a congregation. What are the risks of disclosing or not disclosing identity?

Day 4: Esther 5–8
Counterplot

Once Esther accepts her role as a champion for her people, the narrative moves quickly to resolution. The action of the narrative is connected with banquets. The opening banquet in Esther 1 leads to Queen Vashti's expulsion. In the second half of the narrative, Esther's disclosure of her identity takes place through two banquets that she prepares for the king. The book concludes with the festival banquet of Purim, celebrating God's salvation of the people (Esth 9).

At the beginning of the story in Esther 1, the king and his queen are at separate banquets, and he sends a request to her, which she refuses. In the second round of banquets, the queen Esther invites the king and Haman to one banquet for the purpose of inviting them to a second one, where she makes her request known. Esther's decision to identify with her people leads to Haman's demise and allows for an edict that permits Jews to defend themselves against any who would attack them. This self-defense looks like revenge at the end of the book, and it raises concerns about how the experience of oppression can lead to similarly oppressive behavior when the power is reversed.

In an environment where God isn't readily apparent, how do we as readers discern God's presence in the story of Esther?

Day 5: Song of Songs 1–2; 4:1-7; 5:10-16
Love unplugged

"Set me as a seal over your heart . . . for love is as strong as death" (Song 8:6). The Song of Songs means "the best of all songs." It is about unrestrained, passionate love. The lovers talk to each other, and their dialogue celebrates the joy of being together. When they are apart, theirs is the language of longing, and their words fill the void created by the absence of the dearly loved partner.

It's hard to ignore the lush imagery of this poetry and how it evokes Eden's garden—the place where humanity and God were together. In the ancient Near East, gardens were walled for protection and often elevated. For this reason, in biblical tradition the garden also becomes a metaphor for Jerusalem, the holy city on a hill, where the temple is the point of contact for God and God's people.

The unmitigated passion and longing of this poetry has caused Jewish and Christian interpreters to gravitate toward allegorical and symbolic readings, seeing this human love as symbolic of the divine-human relationship. However, the experience of human passion and longing is a fitting lens through which to explore the power of relationship and the meaning of the covenant. Through the Song of Songs, we see with new eyes the depth of the agony we experience when we are separated from our dearly loved partner. The experiences of exile and life in the diaspora were challenging not only because of all the practical uncertainties. They were also times of deep longing for what was lost and for restoration of union with God in the garden, that place where the lovers are unencumbered and free to satisfy their desires.

Jot down some feelings or images that describe a time when you were passionate about a relationship, or deeply loved through a relationship. Now imagine what it would feel like to physically lose a relationship with that person. List some words that describe this feeling.

Day 6: Song of Songs 8:6-7a
Covenant Meditation: God loves you.

Before you begin today's reading practice, make the space in which you will be reading as quiet and separated from distractions as possible. You will be using Song of Songs 8:6-7a as the text for your reading. Locate these verses and mark the place so that when you begin, it is easy to find. Now get as comfortable as you can, choosing a position in which you can be most relaxed and at ease with your imagination. If this means that you would rather sit or lie on the floor, don't hesitate to do so. Sometimes a change in posture or position can help us to move into a new way of living with God's word. (In several psalms we read about thinking of God's word as the psalmist lies in bed at night.)

Now, recall that our theme for this week is "Faithful Love." Our readings led us into stories and poetry about God's faithful love for human beings and about faithful love between humans arising from a deep, faithful love for God. Covenant love is at the center of our love for each other and for God.

With this in mind, now read aloud Song of Songs 8:6-7a. When you have finished this first reading, imagine that these verses are God's request to you. Imagine God speaking these words to you, describing the love God has for you, asking that you set God's love for you as a seal upon your heart. Read the verses again, aloud or silently, as though you are hearing God telling you about the depth of love God has for you. Take this to heart. Live as deeply as you can with this idea of how much God loves you.

Now take a minute or two of silence and rest, then read these verses again, aloud or silently. But this time, let this be your prayer in response to God. Offer these same words back to God, asking that God place your life and love upon the divine heart so that you might grow in your love for God, one love bound to the other. Ask God to help you grow in such unrelenting, unquenchable love for God and for others. Let your imagination help you form an image of this fierce and passionate love that you and God have for each other, out of which your love for others and for all creation can live and move and have presence. Close with "Amen."

Group Meeting Experience

Ruth 1:8-18 | *Solemn promise for life*

On the way back to Bethlehem, the widowed Naomi offers her widowed daughters-in-law a unique opportunity. She gives them the option to return home to their families of origin. Ruth responds with a solemn promise that expresses her covenant commitment.

1. Look for repetition in this passage. Are there actions or motifs that we have seen in other parts of the Ruth narrative? How often do we see terms like "return" or "go back"? What themes does the repetition evoke?

2. Ruth's solemn promise to Naomi is a turning point in the narrative. What are the elements of Ruth's promise, and how do they reflect the aspects of the marriage covenant Ruth made when she married Mahlon and joined the family of Elimelech and Naomi? What do the elements of the covenant tell us about the "family values" of the time? In other words, based on what Ruth promises, what are the markers of family?

3. The exchange between Naomi and her daughters-in-law takes place in between Moab and Bethlehem. What is the significance of this location?

4. Ruth seals her promise by pledging, "May the LORD do this to me and more so if even death separates me from you" (Ruth 1:17). When she invokes this curse, she makes it impossible for Naomi to send her back. What are the theological implications of this part of the story? How would Israelite audiences have responded to a Moabite making a solemn pledge in the Lord's name?

5. How do the major women characters in this story, Ruth and Naomi, reflect the love, loyalty, and faithfulness that exemplify true covenant relationships in the biblical world?

SIGNS OF FAITHFUL LOVE

Covenant people say to God, "Wherever you go,
I will go. Wherever you stay, I will stay."

Luke and Acts

THE SPIRIT-LED COMMUNITY
To change our hearts and lives and tell others about it

Bible Readings

Day 1: Luke 1:1–4:30

Day 2: Luke 10:25-37; 13; 15; 16:19–17:19; 18:1-17; 19:1-10

Day 3: Luke 22–24

Day 4: Acts 1–4

Day 5: Acts 8:1b–11:18

Day 6: Covenant Meditation on Acts 2:42-47

Day 7: Group Meeting Experience with Luke 4:14-30

Covenant Prayer

For all who feel like God's saving love is reserved for a select few

I really am learning that God doesn't show partiality to one group of people over another. (Acts 10:34)

For those who use their gifts to help and bring people together in a spirit of compassion, justice, and sharing

Treat people in the same way that you want them to treat you. (Luke 6:31)

OUR
LONGING FOR
RELATIONSHIP

We are afraid of strangers and people who are different from us.

LUKE AND ACTS

You can see how Matthew, Mark, and Luke share some of the same materials by studying the CEB Gospel Parallels.

Luke's Gospel presents Jesus Christ as the savior who announces and brings God's salvation. This salvation is concerned with physical, social, and spiritual well-being.

The Acts of the Apostles adds to the gospel story by describing Jesus' ministry as it continues in the lives of his followers. In Acts, the Holy Spirit creates communities united in faith and service and leads followers outward to bring the good news about Jesus into many cultural settings.

As the openings to both books (Luke 1:1-4; Acts 1:1-2) make clear, Acts was written as a sequel to Luke. The same person composed both of these books, probably between the years 80 and 95 CE. In many ways the two books connect to each other in their themes and emphases. For example, both have the whole Roman Empire in view, and they see the Christian gospel as something relevant for the whole world—at least the world known to people living under Roman rule. While introducing John the Baptist, Luke mentions the emperor and other regional rulers (Luke 3:1-2). In Luke's Gospel, Jesus brings God's salvation to "all peoples" (Luke 2:29-32). Acts begins with Jesus' followers huddled together in Jerusalem, but ends with Paul in the imperial capital, Rome, awaiting an audience with the emperor. In between, the gospel travels into major cities and through remote areas across the empire. (See the map in the back of the *CEB Study Bible* for an overview of where Paul traveled.)

Even as Luke and Acts tell of salvation brought to new and sometimes exotic places, they insist that the source of this salvation is very familiar. Luke's opening chapters use phrases and themes from the Old Testament to reassert God's continuing faithfulness. Jesus speaks of his ministry—and his death and resurrection—as fulfilling scripture. Characters in Acts also frequently cite Old Testament scripture to make sense of what God has done through Jesus and what God is continuing to do in their midst. Luke and Acts present themselves as the continuation of the stories about God that began in the Old Testament.

Although Luke shares much in common with Matthew and Mark, the perception of Jesus in Luke's Gospel is quite distinctive. A good amount of the material in Luke 3:1–9:50, as well as most of the account of Jesus' final fateful visit to Jerusalem in Luke 19:28–23:56, resembles passages found in Matthew and Mark. At the same time, most of the stories in Luke 9:51–19:27, a section initiated by a statement about Jesus' determination to travel to Jerusalem, appear in no other Gospel. There readers find, among other things, several noteworthy parables and challenging teachings about wealth and possessions.

Luke names Jesus as "Lord," "savior," "Messiah" (or "Christ"), "God's Son," and other familiar titles. This Gospel also places a special accent on Jesus' identity as a prophet. Jesus, in Luke 4:25-27, compares himself to great prophets in the Old Testament (see also Acts 3:22). He performs deeds, such as raising a widow's only son from the dead, that recall these prophets (Luke 7:11-17; compare 1 Kgs 17:17-24). He also utters a lament about Jerusalem in Luke 19:41-43 with words reminiscent of Old Testament prophets. Depicting Jesus and his followers as prophets emphasizes his role as one who announces God's actions on behalf of God's people. Sometimes this prophecy announces the upending of the status quo (as when Mary, Jesus' mother, speaks of the overturning of social orders in Luke 1:51-53). Sometimes the prophecy calls for changed hearts and lives (Luke 5:32; 13:3), imploring people to adopt a new perspective on God and their accountability to God.

Jesus announces God's salvation frequently during meals. See Luke 5:27-31; 7:36-50; 10:38-42; 24:36-49.

Jesus announces God's salvation frequently in intimate settings and for the sake of those who most need God's helping love and power in their lives. Many scenes occur around communal meals. This Gospel includes nineteen references to meals. Often these settings provide opportunities for transformations to occur, or for outsiders to be recognized as coming into a group of insiders. Similarly, no other Gospel pays as much attention to people who lacked power in ancient society. Frequently in Luke, Jesus speaks about or interacts with women, the poor, the ill, and the outcasts.

When we move into Acts, Jesus, after his ascent into heaven, bestows the Holy Spirit on his followers, empowering them for ministry and knitting them together into communities of mutual care and worship. Just as Luke gives special attention to the roles of the Holy Spirit and prayer in Jesus' ministry, Acts regularly reminds readers that worship, prayer, and service are aspects of Spirit-led churches. Jesus' impact on the world doesn't end or pause when he ascends into heaven after his resurrection. Rather, his story continues in the Christian communities that live out and proclaim his salvation, guided by the Holy Spirit. Even when these groups and their leaders encounter resistance from powerful people—which happens often in Acts—the Lord's word is nevertheless proclaimed, sometimes in unexpected ways.

In Acts, the Spirit empowers all Christians to be prophets (Acts 2:17-18), interpreters of God's action, of God's salvation on behalf of the whole world. Nevertheless, they do their work without knowing all the answers. Regularly the Spirit surprises them, such as when God brings non-Jews (Gentiles) into the church, the community of God's people (Acts 10:1-18; 15:1-35). The book tells of responsive churches—communities of people who must discern God's leading as they are called to bear witness to Jesus with boldness in their lives.

We learn about the purpose of Luke and Acts in the prologues (Luke 1:1-4; Acts 1:1-2). The books are addressed to a man named Theophilus, about whom nothing else is known. He may have been a patron, someone who commissioned the author to write both books for his or his community's benefit. Even though the author, whom church tradition names as "Luke," is aware of other Gospels and was himself not an eyewitness of Jesus' ministry, still he deems it worthwhile to provide another account. He does this for the sake of Theophilus and other believers, to give them "confidence in the soundness of the instruction" (Luke 1:4) they have already received. This indicates that Luke writes about Jesus and the early church, not necessarily to convince skeptics, but so that he might strengthen existing faith.

Luke and Acts don't understand personal religious commitments or spiritual lives as being separate from who people are as members of society and participants in a community. People changed by Jesus become part of his ongoing work in the world.

Day 1: Luke 1:1–4:30

Jesus fulfills hopes and confounds expectations.

The first two chapters of Luke describe Jesus coming to people who are eager for and amazed by his arrival. Three characters in particular respond to what God is doing in these events by singing songs (Luke 1:46-55, 67-79; 2:28-32). Each song is composed of phrases and themes taken from the Old Testament. The songs are prophecies because they celebrate God's will and name God's activity. In the conceptions and births of John and Jesus, Luke asserts that God is doing a new thing, giving light and guidance (Luke 1:79) that brings about salvation for "all peoples," both Jews and non-Jews, or Gentiles (Luke 2:31-32). At the same time, these actions of God are hardly new. God has, in the past, regularly shown mercy (Luke 1:50) and has made reliable promises to God's people (Luke 1:54-55, 72-75). Luke tells the next chapter of an ongoing story.

In Luke 3, John's ministry begins. He calls for changed hearts and lives (repentance) and promises judgment. In the following chapter, Jesus must discern what it means for him to be "God's Son." Will Jesus seek privilege and glory, or will he submit himself to a different way? Luke then introduces Jesus' public ministry with a story of an incident in his hometown. The scripture Jesus reads and the comments he makes serve as a kind of mission statement for his ministry in Luke.

What has Jesus come to do? Why do the people of Nazareth turn on him?

Day 2: Luke 10:25-37; 13; 15; 16:19–17:19; 18:1-17; 19:1-10

Jesus proclaims God's kingdom.

Sample some of the most loved—and most challenging—passages in Luke's Gospel. Together, they provide an overview of the topics Jesus addresses in his teachings. Note in particular how outcasts or powerless people figure in these stories.

In what ways is Jesus merciful and reassuring? In what ways is he, like the prophets, hard on those who misuse power and wealth to oppress others?

It's common to read stories like these and ask ourselves, "How should we be more like Jesus?" or, "How can we act like the people Jesus commends?" While those questions are useful, consider this one instead: "What does Jesus promise in these stories?" That is, think about what Jesus says is true about himself, people, life, and God.

Day 3: Luke 22–24

Jesus, the rejected prophet, dies and rises again.

Every Gospel tells about Jesus' death and resurrection, but Luke tells these stories in several unique ways.

How would you describe the mood around Jesus' crucifixion in Luke?

Luke mentions the presence of people who support Jesus and mourn his death (Luke 23:27, 48). Only in Luke does one of the criminals appeal to Jesus on the cross (Luke 23:39-43). Jesus promises salvation to him, even as both of them suffer miserable deaths. Jesus dies speaking words of trust in God (Luke 23:46). This message demonstrates his faithfulness, even on the cross.

Luke, along with John, contains the most stories about the resurrected Jesus' appearances to his followers. Notice how Jesus, risen from the dead, is both hidden from his followers and recognizable to them. Their belief doesn't come automatically. Their eyes have to be opened. Their memories have to be jogged. They need to encounter him directly and personally.

How do you recognize Jesus directly and personally two thousand years after his resurrection?

As the Gospel draws to a close, Jesus calls his followers "witnesses" of all that has occurred (Luke 24:48). The book of Acts will reaffirm the importance of that term. The word *witness* brings to mind legal settings.

What does it mean to bear witness to Jesus?

Jesus instructs people to proclaim "a change of heart and life" (or repentance) for "forgiveness" (or "release"; recall Luke 4:18) from sins.

How do you think forgiveness or release stems from Jesus' death and resurrection?

Day 4: Acts 1–4

Jesus' followers receive power from the Holy Spirit.

Acts, a story packed with adventures, begins with waiting. Jesus commissions his followers as his "witnesses," not just where they are but also as far as "the end of the earth" (Acts 1:8). But first they must wait for the Holy Spirit's power.

What does it mean to associate the Holy Spirit with "power"? What kind of power is Jesus talking about?

The Spirit arrives, with much fanfare, in Acts 2. This is the first of many stories in Acts in which the Spirit launches new movements in the church's life and witness. Peter announces that the strange events of Pentecost give evidence of the Spirit, a Spirit promised to all members of the community (Acts 2:17-18). The coming of the Spirit, claims Peter, is a sign that Jesus has ascended to God's right side, meaning he now possesses all God's authority over creation. Mention of Jesus' death prompts the crowd to react, and Peter tells them, "Change your hearts and lives" (Acts 2:37-38). As the chapter ends, the Spirit creates a community unified by its fellowship, worship, and charity. Acts 2 indicates the Spirit's presence outdoors as people proclaim the gospel, and indoors as the church organizes its common life.

What is the source in your church fellowship, worship, and charity? Are you comfortable with speaking about the Spirit inside and outside the church?

In Acts 3–4, we glimpse the church in action, continuing Jesus' ministry of healing and teaching, describing Jesus as fulfilling what God promised in advance, and encountering opposition from religious authorities. A major theme in these chapters is the power of Jesus' "name" and God's "word."

What does it mean to you to bear "the name" of Christ? How is the message or good news about Jesus "God's word" for you?

Day 5: Acts 8:1*b*–11:18
Unlikely newcomers join the church.

> **Optional:** *An additional video retelling the story of Peter and Cornelius is available for download from* **CovenantBibleStudy.com**.

The book of Acts is full of surprises, including events that seem to catch the people in the story unaware and that are interpreted as God's actions. This section of Acts begins with Jesus' followers having to leave Jerusalem in response to harassment. What might look like a setback quickly becomes an occasion for the church to expand. Samaritans, people usually considered enemies or rivals of those from Judea (where Jerusalem was) and Galilee, respond positively to the gospel message. So, too, in an astonishing scene, does an official of the royal court in Ethiopia. Then Jesus reaches out directly to Saul (later known as Paul), the church's archenemy. Just when things couldn't get much stranger, God prompts Peter and an official in the Roman military to find each other, resulting in the salvation of Cornelius and his household. Acts 10:1–11:18 is a pivotal scene, told with much repetition and great care to make its point. As a result, the church in Jerusalem (which at this point appears to be composed entirely of Jews) declares that God (not Peter) acted to give salvation to Gentiles, bringing about in them changed hearts and lives (repentance). As a result, the community of Jesus' followers would never be the same.

As you read these stories, note all of the places where Acts describes God, Jesus, or the Spirit doing something. Note also where characters in the story name God, Jesus, or the Spirit as the agents behind events or ideas.

Why do faithful people understand God as the primary force leading the community of believers in new directions? Give an example of an event where God was plainly the cause of what happened.

Day 6: Acts 2:42-47

Covenant Meditation: Teaching, prayers, and shared meals

We will experience a reading from Acts through the spiritual gift of imagination. In the introduction for this week, our author writes, "People changed by Jesus become part of his ongoing work in the world." Since the beginning of the church, Christians have helped each other figure out and grow into what it means to live in community day by day. Our text for this time of spiritual reading invites us to see and join with these early brothers and sisters of faith.

Turn to Acts 2:42-47 and mark this reading so that you can find it easily. Before you begin to read, close your eyes, quiet your breath, and set aside distractions as best you can. Then, when you are ready, read these verses slowly and imagine yourself as part of each community activity. Take each phrase and sentence to heart, placing yourself in the community as an active member. What does it look like for you to "devote" yourself to the apostles' teaching? What do you bring to the meals? Who else is at the table? For what are you all praying? Who is offering the prayers?

What does it look like to experience with others "awe" for what God is doing? What are community members sharing? What do they need from each other? What do you have to share and to whom do you give it?

As you slowly work through this reading, take time to notice what you see (colors, expressions, interactions); what you hear (voices, laughter, table noises); and what you smell and taste and touch. Then close this time of reflection by examining your thoughts and feelings about this community of believers. What caught your attention? What troubled you? What will you take with you from this reading, from this community to whom we are connected by faith?

When you are finished, offer a prayer of gratitude for these brothers and sisters who, like us, had to find their way as Christ-followers. Offer as well a prayer of gratitude for a community of faith that has helped to shape your spiritual life.

Group Meeting Experience

Luke 4:14-30 | Jesus preaches in his synagogue.

Following his temptation in the wilderness, Jesus returns to Galilee "in the power of the Spirit" (Luke 4:14). He heads to his hometown of Nazareth, where a Sabbath visit to the synagogue finds him doing what he's always done: reading from the scriptures. As he reads aloud the scroll from Isaiah the prophet, he reaffirms God's clear and present favor for those living with impoverishment, bondage, blindness, and oppression. Then, in his address, Jesus extends this favored status to Gentiles outside the traditional boundaries of the covenant people—and it almost costs him his life.

1. What do we learn about the role of the Lord's Spirit in Luke 4:14-18? Why is it important to understand that the Holy Spirit is active in Jesus' ministry? What does it mean for us, then, that we possess the same Holy Spirit? How does the Holy Spirit assist the church as we work on God's behalf in the wider world and seek to be a community that embodies mutual love and support? How does your understanding of the Holy Spirit, as the book of Acts has informed you this week, affect your reading of Luke 4:14-30?

2. The scripture Jesus reads in the synagogue comes mostly from Isaiah 61:1-2a, with a portion of Isaiah 58:6 added. The release and liberation spoken about in these passages strikes an echo with the "Jubilee year" described in Leviticus 25:8-55. Jesus speaks in Luke 4, then, of fulfilling themes that already have deep significance in his people's hopes and memories. How would you summarize or reword these themes? What do these themes mean to you? What do you think he means when he says, "Today, this scripture has been fulfilled just as you heard it" (Luke 4:21)?

3. The scriptures from Isaiah that Jesus reads describe people being restored. What does it mean to you to be restored or released? What does a community of restored people look like to you? What challenges does such a community face? Is there any cause for worry in these images of powerless people suddenly becoming empowered? How might such radical transformations affect a wider society, or the world at large?

4. The people of Jesus' hometown, those who probably know him very well, try to kill him at the end of this incident. What motivates them to do this? Why does Jesus seem uninterested in diffusing

the tension or lessening the offense they feel? What do these people expect from him, and why won't he give them what they want? Where is the root of the misunderstanding or hostility in this passage?

SIGNS OF FAITHFUL LOVE

Covenant people rejoice and multiply when the Holy Spirit forms us into a dynamic and growing community. We grow by revealing the good news of Jesus Christ to unexpected groups of people.

2 Samuel, 1 and 2 Kings

LEADERSHIP
Potential and peril of leadership

Bible Readings

Day 1: 2 Samuel 7; 9; 11–12

Day 2: 1 Kings 11–13

Day 3: 1 Kings 17–19; 21

Day 4: 2 Kings 17–19

Day 5: 2 Kings 22–25

Day 6: Covenant Meditation on 2 Kings 5:1-14

Day 7: Group Meeting Experience with 2 Samuel 7:1-17

Covenant Prayer

For those who lead powerful governments and institutions

He has told you, human one, what is good and what the LORD requires from you: to do justice, embrace faithful love, and walk humbly with your God. (Micah 6:8)

For those who are at the mercy of power brokers

My God, rescue me from the power of the wicked; rescue me from the grip of the wrongdoer and the oppressor because you are my hope, Lord. (Psalm 71:4-5a)

OUR LONGING FOR RELATIONSHIP

Staying faithful to the covenant is tested through our ambitions and desires, our illusion of self-sufficiency, the idols of culture, and internal family conflicts.

KINGS

In 586 BCE, Babylonia's King Nebuchadnezzar and his army destroyed the city of Jerusalem. This destruction included not only the wall around the city, the houses, and the palace, but also God's temple, which had been built by Solomon, David's son. Many of the inhabitants of Jerusalem and the surrounding countryside were killed during the siege. The elite were forcibly exiled to Babylon. Most of those exiled died in that foreign land, far removed from their former homes, their former ways of life, and their former religious traditions. It's a tragedy that is difficult for us to appreciate. The effects of Jerusalem's destruction are certainly hard to overestimate.

The disaster of the destruction was made worse because it simply wasn't supposed to happen. The kingdom of Israel was established in a real and vigorous way by David, someone specially chosen and dearly loved by God. Because of God's particular regard for David, he established a covenant with David, promising him not only that God would bless him and make him great but that God would also provide a dynasty after David. God also made one additional promise in that covenant: David's dynasty would be eternal. There would always be one of David's descendants sitting on his throne in Jerusalem. Regardless of the faithfulness or disloyalty of any of the descendants, the covenant would never fail (2 Sam 7). The dynasty of David—and, by implication, David's city—would last forever. However, in 586 BCE Nebuchadnezzar's army destroyed the land and put the promise in doubt.

The books of 2 Samuel and 1 and 2 Kings address the strengths and weaknesses of the Davidic monarchy and its leadership of the people of Israel. How is it that God entered into an eternal covenant with David and his sons? How do David and his descendants successfully rule such a powerful and long-lasting kingdom? Why do they assume such a central place in the lives of God's people?

On the other hand, how could Jerusalem fall to the Babylonians? What are the causes of that destruction? Not merely the immediate causes, such as the rise of Babylonia or the weakness of Judah's final king, Zedekiah. Deeper causes stretch throughout Israel's entire history, all the way back to David and his promised son, Solomon. Are those causes only political and economic, or are they also religious and social? How do Israel's political and religious leaders and the people of Israel themselves contribute to or slow down the deterioration of the nation?

The books of 2 Samuel and 1 and 2 Kings wrestle with the nature of leadership of all types: social, religious, and political. A common refrain throughout the books is the evaluation of each of the kings who did "what was right in the LORD's eyes" (that is, keeping their covenant commitments) or "what was evil in the LORD's eyes" (that is, disregarding the covenant).

These stories about Israel's kings are far from simplistic statements about who was good and who was bad. These books illustrate again and again that there is more to a good leader than simply obeying a set of instructions, and more to a bad leader than simply not doing whatever God's instructions state. Leadership involves and combines many different qualities: justice, mercy, compromise, determination, authority, humility, an awareness of the "big picture," and attention to detail. Starting with the crowning of David and ending with the torture and death of Zedekiah, these stories offer us a way to wrestle with the purpose and strategies of leadership.

The stories about the kings also help us understand the prophetic figures who provide an alternative model of leadership that confronts the ruler on behalf of the powerless. The prophets play a major role in these stories, delivering God's word to the kings of Israel and Judah and holding them accountable to the covenant. Like the righteous kings, the prophets also are accountable to the covenant life.

Although the stories in 2 Samuel and 1 and 2 Kings present what looks like history, it is a history that is told for a particular purpose. While a modern historian might want to know more about various Assyrian or Babylonian leaders, or about particular political, economic, or social realities of the ancient world, these stories are wrestling with different issues: What does it mean to live in covenant with God? What does faithful, strong leadership look like? What does unfaithful, weak leadership look like? What are the reasons David's kingdom assumed a central place in God's covenant with the people of Israel and endured for centuries? What role do prophetic figures play in Israel's history? And how are we to understand the various reasons why David's kingdom, which was so full of promise and security, became so fragile and was eventually destroyed?

Leadership involves and combines many different qualities: justice, mercy, compromise, determination, authority, humility, an awareness of the "big picture," and attention to detail.

History with a purpose: portrayals of faithful and weak leadership

*For a table with a complete list
of the kings of Israel and Judah,
see the* CEB Study Bible, *OT
page 543.*

Day 1: 2 Samuel 7; 9; 11–12
David's use and abuse of power

The story of 2 Samuel outlines the ways in which David gained the kingship over all Israel and then almost lost it. After Saul's death, David becomes king over his own tribe of Judah in the area to the south and west of the city of Jerusalem (2 Sam 2:1-7). From this area, David wages war against one of Saul's remaining sons, Ishbosheth, who is king over the other tribes that live north of Judah. In turn, Abner, the commanding general of the northern army, as well as Ishbosheth, are assassinated. David, however, denies that he had any knowledge of the plots to kill these two leaders. The people hear David's denial and are pleased that David, by his own account, is innocent of the murders (2 Sam 3–4). After this, David becomes king over the northern tribes (together called Israel) as well. David finally conquers Jerusalem and sets it up as his own city, making Jerusalem the center of political and religious power (2 Sam 5–6).

> **Optional:** *An additional video on David and the peril and promise of faithful leadership is available for download from* **CovenantBibleStudy.com**.

In 2 Samuel 7, God enters into a covenant with David and promises him that his kingdom will last forever, because after David's death God will raise up one of David's sons to rule on his throne. In 2 Samuel 9 we see how David deals with Saul's one remaining son, Mephibosheth, who is lame and can't walk. Is David being merciful or cautious (or both) here?

In 2 Samuel 11–12, we see the inner workings of the affair between David and Bathsheba and of the tragic judgment that it provokes from God. This is an intimate account of the failure of leadership, and the author draws the reader into its personal details. Is the affair as secret as it appears at first glance? Does Uriah know? In what way does David disregard his covenant obligations and what are the consequences? How does God's judgment "fit the crime"?

As you read, consider how the various characters might understand the situation, whether people are being honest or lying, and how people are using whatever power they might have.

How would you evaluate David's leadership, both in his crime and in his response to Nathan's accusation? How does Nathan provide prophetic leadership?

Day 2: 1 Kings 11–13

Loss of Israel

After a long and seemingly prosperous reign, we see Solomon in a negative light here at the end of his life. This is the author's explanation for Solomon's failure to maintain rule over his father David's united kingdom. In chapter 11, Solomon is blamed for disregarding the covenant and for worshipping other gods, the first and most important obligation of the covenant (1 Kgs 11:1-13; compare Deut 5:6-10; 6:4-5). In chapter 12, he is blamed for exploiting the citizens of the north and abusing them through forced labor (1 Kgs 12:1-20).

According to Deuteronomy 17:14-20—a passage that is closely linked to the stories in Kings—a king of Israel was prohibited from having many horses, which probably refers to having a personal army. He was denied a personal treasury. And he couldn't have many wives, probably because intermarrying with the daughters of foreign rulers symbolized the making of treaties with foreign nations. Deuteronomy seems to warn that kings with great power tend to abuse that power for personal ends—as we saw in the reading for Day 1. While 1 Kings 1–10 tells the story of Solomon's reign in positive terms, it's also clear that he builds up his personal army with more than forty thousand horses (1 Kgs 4:26-28; 10:26-29), that he has so much money that he makes "silver as common as stones" (1 Kgs 10:27), and that he has placed some of his citizens into forced labor (1 Kgs 4:6). Yes, he had wisdom (1 Kgs 3:1-15). But which influenced his rule more, his wisdom or his personal power? By the end of his life, it became clear: His absolute power had corrupted him absolutely.

As you read these stories, think about what strengths and weaknesses in Solomon's leadership are reflected in his own son, Rehoboam, as well as in Jeroboam, the son who becomes the new king over the northern tribes of Israel. Prophetic leaders—Ahijah the man of God and the old prophet—also play an important role in these stories.

Considering Nathan in the previous readings and the prophets in these readings, do we still need prophets to hold rulers accountable for their covenant obligations? What covenant obligations in our community right now are in need of a prophet?

Day 3: 1 Kings 17–19; 21
King versus prophet

These stories are set in the northern kingdom of Israel and center around the prophet Elijah and the king Ahab. Ahab, like Solomon in the previous reading, also has a wife who is the daughter of a foreign king and sponsors great building projects of a religious nature. Like Solomon, he worships other gods, breaking the first obligation of the covenant (1 Kgs 18), and abuses his power over his subjects (1 Kgs 21). In both instances, the prophet Elijah stands up to the king and demands that Ahab keep his covenant obligations.

On Mount Carmel, Elijah summons all the prophets of the foreign gods Baal and Asherah to a contest, a contest in which Israel's God prevails. In spite of this victory, however, and in spite of the end of the drought, Elijah is terrified by a threat by Jezebel. He runs to Horeb, the mountain where Moses and the Israelites witnessed God's presence and received the Ten Commandments and the Instruction (Torah) about how to live in covenant (Deut 5–9; compare Exod 20–24). Here God appears also to Elijah (but not in the way God did to Moses and Israel) and gives him instructions (but not like those God gave to Moses and Israel).

When Ahab tries to seize the family farm of one of his subjects, Elijah stands up to him again for abusing his power (1 Kgs 21). Clearly, Elijah is presented as an opponent to Ahab and Jezebel. As you read these stories, notice how the kind of leadership exemplified by Elijah is both similar to and different from that of Ahab's leadership.

Does this similarity or difference between Ahab and Elijah tell us anything about the strengths and weaknesses, as well as the purposes and dangers, of leadership?

Day 4: 2 Kings 17–19
The fall of Samaria and the northern kingdom

In 722 BCE, the army of the Assyrian Empire came against the northern kingdom of Israel. The Assyrians destroyed its capital city of Samaria, killed some of its inhabitants, and forcibly moved others back to Assyria, settling them throughout the country. We are told that this occurred because Israel's King Hoshea withheld the yearly tribute that the Assyrian king demanded and made an alliance with Egypt, Assyria's enemy (2 Kgs 17:4). Yet this reason isn't the one that is highlighted by the reading for today. Instead, the text includes a long sermon outlining the various reasons why Israel collapsed from the inside out (2 Kgs 17:7-41). In contrast, the story is also told about Hezekiah, who is held up as a positive role model, and about how God miraculously rescues the kingdom of Judah from an Assyrian attack (2 Kgs 18–19).

The covenant relationship established in Deuteronomy (see Episode 8) provides the lens for evaluating the behavior of the people and their kings. As you read about the destruction of Samaria and the reasons given for it and about Hezekiah and the rescue of Jerusalem, notice how the character of Hezekiah is contrasted with the inhabitants of Israel throughout the long sermon.

What are the specific differences between Hezekiah and the people? What role do prophetic leaders play?

Day 5: 2 Kings 22–25
The fall of Jerusalem and the southern kingdom

In 586 BCE, the army of the Babylonian Empire, under King Nebuchadnezzar, came against the city of Jerusalem, destroyed it, and exiled all but the poorest people to Babylon. The importance of this event and the end of the Davidic dynasty is impossible to overstate in the way it influenced Israelite and Jewish religion and theology, and in the formation of holy scripture itself. The readings for today outline the events of those final decades of Judah's kingdom with an eye toward understanding how such a tragic event occurred.

The reading begins in the aftermath of the reigns of Manasseh and Amon, who had sponsored the worship of foreign gods and religious practices against the clear instructions of the covenant. In a counter to this, Josiah reigned and brought about a religious reform based on a scroll that was found in the temple. Josiah, like Hezekiah in the last reading, is presented as a positive character who ushers in a reign of peace and faithfulness to God (2 Kgs 22:1–23:25). Most scholars believe that the scroll found during Josiah's reign was a version of Deuteronomy, or a version of the Torah, which is now the introduction to the Deuteronomistic History (the books of Joshua, Judges, 1 and 2 Samuel, and 1 and 2 Kings).

> **Optional:** *An additional video on exile and hope is available for download from* **CovenantBibleStudy.com**.

The tragic effects of the long history of unfaithfulness, stretching all the way back perhaps to the very start of the Davidic monarchy with Solomon, or perhaps even to David, couldn't be lessened with a few years of faithfulness under Josiah. The weight was too great, and the effects were too enduring. After Josiah's death, the kings who followed were weak, religiously and politically, and they led the country to disaster.

Think of an example of a leader in recent memory who led his or her people into a disaster. Write the leader's name, and write something you would say to that leader.

Day 6: 2 Kings 5:1-14
Covenant Meditation: Who is the leader?

Many of us are conditioned to read and interpret history in a particular and focused way: to gather details. Historical writings in the Bible are often read for the predetermined purpose of getting straight in our minds the names, dates, places, and events that formed the community of our spiritual ancestors. But as we have learned this week, details and facts are only a few of the gifts intended by God through the stories found in 2 Samuel and 1 and

2 Kings. Within these same sacred texts, we are also invited into the contours of human relationships as created and known by God. We witness the good and the not so good, as our forebearers sought to lead faithful lives and worship the God who makes a covenant with us.

You are invited to expect something fresh from these stories. Find 2 Kings 5:1-14. Before you begin to read, recall that God not only encountered the people in this story from our past, all of whom exhibit different qualities of leadership within the faith community; but that God is just as present and engaged during this time of reading and reflecting on this text. The same God is addressing you here and now. Aloud or in silence, offer this prayer: "God, help me to seek and follow those you call to lead."

Now, slowly read 2 Kings 5:1-14. As you read, or reread, make a list of any of the characters' leadership qualities, noting especially those qualities valued by God. Be open to different kinds and forms of leadership, formal and informal, official and behind-the-scenes. Set aside assumptions about leadership that you might be carrying with you to this reading, and look for those qualities that lead to the kind of life desired by God. Review your list. Offer these qualities or characteristics of leadership to God in gratitude and remember those in your community who bring these qualities into your shared life together. Be specific as you let leaders come to mind.

Optional: *An additional video retelling the story of Naaman and Elisha is available for download from* **CovenantBibleStudy.com**.

Group Meeting Experience

2 Samuel 7:1-17 | *Covenant with David*

God makes a covenant with David, promising him that he will become famous, that Israel will live securely, that David himself won't be troubled by any enemies, and that David will have a dynasty. After David's death, one of his own sons will reign in his place, will build a temple for God, and will become God's own son. God further declares that this covenant won't be affected by the obedience or disobedience of the son, but will last forever and be eternal. David will, forever, have a descendant sitting on his throne in Jerusalem.

1. The passage begins with David's wish to build God a permanent house or palace, so that God's holy chest won't stay in a tent. In light of David's character, as seen in the reading for Day 1, why might David want to do this? Are there positive reasons why David might want to do this? Are there selfish reasons? How does David's initial plan here mirror what else we know about his character?

2. The introduction to the covenant begins with a relatively long section about God's history with Israel (2 Sam 7:5-7), God's history with David (2 Sam 7:8-9a), and God's plans for both (2 Sam 7:9b-11a). Why might the covenant begin this way? What role does this introduction play in the larger speech? Do you see any parallels between these three sections? If so, how do those parallels cause us to think about Israel? David? God?

3. The central point in the promise of the dynasty (2 Sam 7:11b-16) is that the royal line of David's descendants will last forever. The word *forever* appears three times (2 Sam 7:13, 16). The phrase "will never take my faithful love away" emphasizes this (2 Sam 7:15). The phrase "I will establish" has a sense of permanence (2 Sam 7:13), as does the phrase "will be secured" (2 Sam 7:16). Why does the covenant make such a point about the permanence and eternal nature of David's dynasty? If, as pointed out in the general introduction, these texts reached their final form after the destruction of Jerusalem, the palace, and the throne of David, how does this promise read in light of that eventual disaster?

4. The early Christian church believed that Jesus was a descendant of David and "God's Son." How might those early Christians have read and understood this passage?

5. What is the relationship between God's promises and our responsibility to do what we are called to do?

SIGNS OF FAITHFUL LOVE

God is faithful to Covenant people, even when we fall short.
God's faithfulness comes in many forms: in an unexpected mission,
in an unconditional promise, in the unwelcome rebuke of prophets,
and even in the unwanted appearance of our adversaries.

1 and 2 Thessalonians, 1 and 2 Timothy, Titus

GOD'S HOUSEHOLD

To live responsible, changed, and well-ordered lives

Bible Readings

Day 1: 1 Thessalonians 1–5

Day 2: 2 Thessalonians 1–3

Day 3: 1 Timothy 1:1-2; 2–4; 6:1-2, 11-15

Day 4: 2 Timothy 1–4

Day 5: Titus

Day 6: Covenant Meditation on 2 Timothy 3:14-17

Day 7: Group Meeting Experience with 1 Thessalonians 1:2-10

Covenant Prayer

For all who feel discouraged, unimportant, or isolated from friends and family

Know that the LORD is God—he made us; we belong to him. We are his people, the sheep of his own pasture. (Psalm 100:3)

For pastors, teachers, counselors, and spiritual coaches who encourage others in the faith

Brothers and sisters, we must always thank God for you. This is only right because your faithfulness is growing by leaps and bounds, and the love that all of you have for each other is increasing.
(2 Thessalonians 1:3)

OUR LONGING FOR RELATIONSHIP

Often we hurt each other by word and deed in our homes or in our faith communities.

43

PAUL'S LETTERS

The five books in this unit are letters attributed to the apostle Paul, composed over a period of about fifty years. First Thessalonians was probably written around 50 or 51 CE, making it the earliest book of the New Testament. Three of the letters, 1 and 2 Timothy and Titus, were likely written late in the first century CE or early in the second, while the date of 2 Thessalonians remains uncertain.

Although the letters span a lengthy time period and were written to different communities, they share a concern to encourage the followers of Christ to live lives dedicated to God (1 Thess 4:3). As the author tells us, "I'm writing these things to you so that if I'm delayed, you'll know how you should behave in God's household. It is the church of the living God and the backbone and support of the truth" (1 Tim 3:14-15). As we read these letters, we might imagine ourselves flipping through the pages of a family scrapbook, catching occasional and one-sided glimpses of the stories and images preserved there. We will sometimes need to read between the lines in order to understand what is going on in the communities represented in these letters.

In the first decades after the crucifixion and resurrection, the followers of Jesus gathered for worship and fellowship in houses belonging to wealthier members of each community. Attending these gatherings were believers from a wide cross section of the society: rich and poor, slave and free, women and men, Jews and Gentiles. We can imagine from our own experience, as well as from our knowledge of Paul's letters and other New Testament writings, that it wasn't always easy to live in these "cross-cultural" communities, especially when social conventions differed for different sets of people.

Like other teachers of his day, Paul and his companions wrote letters to offer guidance and encouragement to these gathered communities. In a world without high-speed travel, telephones, Internet, or text messages, letters functioned as a substitute for the actual presence of the writer. Because most people in the first century were unable to read or write, these letters would have been read aloud to the communities to which they were addressed. Letters were a way not only to convey information or to stay in touch, but also to express concern, offer instruction, correct misunderstandings, and provide encouragement.

In the first century, letters were a way not only to stay in touch or to convey information, but also to express concern, offer instruction, correct misunderstandings, and provide encouragement.

For a complete chart of Paul's ministry and writing, see the CEB *Study Bible, NT page 244.*

1 AND 2 THESSALONIANS

Thessalonica was a large city in northern Greece, located at a major crossroads. The population included both Jews and Gentiles, although the young church was predominantly Gentile (they "turned to God from idols"; 1 Thess 1:9). They faced a challenge shared by believers of nearly every time and place: how to live faithfully in a political, religious, and cultural setting that doesn't necessarily share the church's values and commitments.

In what ways does your own church or faith community face a similar challenge? How have you resolved that challenge?

Paul himself had faced "a lot of opposition" and was "publicly insulted," but he reminds the Thessalonians that instead of trying to please people, he and his companions "are trying to please God" (1 Thess 2:2-5). The Thessalonians are in a similar situation, having "suffered the same things from your own people" as the churches in Judea did from theirs (1 Thess 2:14). First Thessalonians demonstrates Paul's warm regard and encouragement for this community. God has given them what they need to live faithfully in the face of their difficulties: They are loved and chosen by God (1 Thess 1:4), and God's word is working in them (1 Thess 2:13), even as they are striving "to live lives worthy of the God who is calling [them] into his own kingdom and glory" (1 Thess 2:12). Paul is delighted to learn of their faithfulness (1 Thess 3:8), and he prompts them to continue encouraging each other and building each other up.

Second Thessalonians suggests that life together in God's household is more difficult when people disagree about how to make sense of a hostile world. The first chapter encourages a community that is facing conflict and suffering from "all the harassments and trouble that you have put up with" (2 Thess 1:4). Using stark terms ("blazing fire" and "the penalty of eternal destruction"), the letter asserts that God's justice will prevail, although it won't be revealed until Jesus returns (2 Thess 1:7-10).

Then, as now, some people thought that Jesus' return ("the day of the Lord") was already happening. From our perspective, two thousand years later, it is impossible to be certain how to interpret some of the details found in the letter, such as "the person who is lawless" in 2 Thessalonians 2:3-12. However, it is clear that harassment of the church doesn't mean that the end is here. The letter offers encouragement and support, reminding readers that "our Lord

Life together in God's household is more difficult when people disagree about how to make sense of a hostile world.

45

Jesus Christ himself and God our Father, loved us and through grace gave us eternal comfort and a good hope" (2 Thess 2:16).

Interpreters are divided about whether 2 Thessalonians was written by Paul and his associates (2 Thess 1:1) or rather by a later author writing in Paul's name. Letter-writers sometimes wrote in another name in order to lend weight and authority to their words.

1 AND 2 TIMOTHY AND TITUS

Collectively called the Pastoral Letters since at least the early eighteenth century, the letters addressed to Timothy and Titus discuss matters of behavior, church structure, and leadership. They are especially concerned with "sound teaching" (Titus 2:1) and how to live a godly life as a member of God's household. For example, 1 Timothy and Titus include explicit instructions for women and men, including slaves (1 Tim 2:8-15; 6:1-2; Titus 2:1-10), while 2 Timothy suggests behaviors and people to avoid (2 Tim 2:22–3:9). These instructions seem to reflect the customs and practices that were common in their day.

In what ways should (or shouldn't) those cultural practices apply today? How might the church decide which practices to eliminate and which ones to keep?

Notice the qualifications for various church leaders. Some debate how organized the early churches were, and this is reflected in the different translations of terms. Should *episkopē* be translated as "bishop" (indicating a highly formalized office) or just "supervisor" (as in the CEB)?

Most interpreters are convinced that all three letters were written sometime after Paul's death (in part because their vocabulary and theology reflect other writings from the second century CE). Does the issue of authorship affect your understanding of the letter or its usefulness for building up the church? Why or why not?

Day 1: 1 Thessalonians 1–5
Encouragement for faithful living

As you read 1 Thessalonians, watch for the ways that Paul builds up the community and indicates his care for and connection to them—for example, in the opening thanksgiving (1 Thess 1:2-10) and in the prayer (1 Thess 3:6-13). Note also the many times Paul uses words like *encourage* and *love*. What impact do you think Paul's language would have on a gathered community that was facing opposition from other people in their city and region?

Especially beautiful and comforting is Paul's message to those whose loved ones have died: "Brothers and sisters, we want you to know about people who have died so that you won't mourn like others who don't have any hope" (1 Thess 4:13). Notice that Paul *never* tells them not to mourn. He absolutely expects Christians to mourn, and he acknowledges the awful pain of separation. But Christian mourning is shaped by the movement toward hope, because we know and trust that the separation isn't ultimate.

If you have lost someone you love, in what ways do Paul's words provide encouragement for you?

One of the ways that Paul shows his solidarity with the Thessalonians is by offering himself as an example: not to brag about himself, but to let them know that he understands the challenges of living out one's faith in difficult circumstances. He encourages them to live "lives worthy of the God who is calling you" (1 Thess 2:12) and to "continue encouraging each other and building each other up, just like you are doing already" (1 Thess 5:11).

What are some of the ways that you can encourage others to remain faithful? What are some of the ways that others encourage you?

Day 2: 2 Thessalonians 1–3
Harassed

Harassment caused some Thessalonian believers to assume that Jesus would return right away, or that he had already come (2 Thess 2:1-3). This was a source of confusion in the church. If you believed that the world would end tomorrow or next week, what would you do? How would that expectation affect your choices and your relationships? Would you quit your job? Among the Thessalonians, it appears that some people stopped working or even taking care of themselves (because they thought the end of the world had come), which meant that others in the community had to pick up the slack (2 Thess 3:6-15). This was a crisis situation for a community that needed to stick together in the face of serious opposition from outside.

The letter promises that no matter what happens, God will give strength to endure (2 Thess 3:3-5; compare 2 Thess 2:17), so that the church might continue to express God's love (2 Thess 3:5; 1:3). Today we occasionally hear dire predictions for the end of the world, but most people don't expect the imminent return of Jesus.

Have you suffered or been harassed by others in your desire to "live a holy life in Christ Jesus" (2 Tim 3:12)? How did you experience God's grace in those situations?

Day 3: 1 Timothy 1:1-2; 2–4; 6:1-2, 11-15
Discernment

First Timothy is an example of a letter from an experienced mentor to his younger charge. The purpose of this instruction is to guide Timothy into a "holy life" (1 Tim 4:7), in part "so that God's name and our teaching won't get a bad reputation" (1 Tim 6:1). Central to the letter is the claim that "Christ Jesus came into the world to save sinners—and I'm the biggest sinner of all" (1 Tim 1:15).

Although 1 Timothy is addressed to an individual, its inclusion in the Bible suggests that early churches found its teaching to be useful for communities as they discerned how to live faithfully in their particular settings. What are some of the teachings from this letter that would nourish the faith community or church of which you are a part? Some of the letter's cultural assumptions (such as slavery as an accepted practice) are no longer accepted by Christians today. Some churches today forbid the ordination of women by citing 1 Timothy 2:8-15.

What do you think about this advice: "A wife should learn quietly with complete submission" (1 Tim 2:11)?

How might you discern which teachings to Timothy (or the behaviors that follow from those teachings) are "reliable" and deserve "complete acceptance" (1 Tim 4:9)?

Day 4: 2 Timothy 1–4
An ethical will

Imprisoned and nearing the end of his life (2 Tim 2:9; 4:6), the author—identified as the apostle Paul—writes to a member of the next generation. Like an "ethical will," the letter testifies to the values that stand at the heart of Paul's faith. It encourages Timothy to "take the things you heard me say . . . and pass them on to faithful people who are also capable of teaching others" (2 Tim 2:2).

Paul points to his own life experiences, particularly his imprisonment and suffering for the sake of the gospel, and sees in them the evidence of God's grace (2 Tim 1:10). He also sees an opportunity to trust in God's power (2 Tim 1:12).

Are there experiences in your life or in the lives of people you know that help you to see God's activity and power?

Paul acknowledges that some people support one's life in the gospel, while other people are destructive to one's life in the gospel and should be avoided (2 Tim 3:1-9). To be sure, he would prefer to have more of the former and fewer of the latter (see, for example, 2 Tim 4:9-18).

Are you hanging out with the right people? People who encourage your faithfulness?

Day 5: Titus

Baptism and the Holy Spirit fuel faithful living. Like 1 and 2 Timothy, the letter to Titus probably represents a period late in the first century or early second, when churches needed to figure out how to organize themselves for the long haul. The letter instructs Titus to appoint elders who will "encourage people with healthy instruction and refute those who speak against it" (Titus 1:9). Instructions for men, women, and slaves tell what it looks like when God's grace "educates us so that we can live sensible, ethical, and godly lives right now by rejecting ungodly lives and the desires of this world" (Titus 2:12). The gospel is proclaimed most clearly when the church is well ordered and when people's behaviors show that they have been changed by God's grace. In this way, the world will know that God, through Christ, "gave himself for us in order to rescue us from every kind of lawless behavior" (Titus 2:14).

Most of the ethical instruction mirrors the teaching of (non-Christian) philosophers and moralists of the day. The difference, however, for the followers of Jesus, is that faithfulness to the new covenant is made possible through baptism and renewal by the Holy Spirit (Titus 3:5).

From all the ethical instructions in Titus, write down one behavior that you want to develop more faithfully in your household.

Day 6: 2 Timothy 3:14-17
Covenant Meditation: Scripture is useful.

Throughout our readings for this week, we learned that the Pastoral Letters written to Timothy, Titus, and the Thessalonians offer guidance on how to "behave" as family members who share responsibilities in God's household. Learning to live together as Christians, and to also live as Christians in a "cross-cultural" world that doesn't share the church's views or values, is no easier today than it was when these letters were first written and read to congregations.

Because these letters were read to congregations, our spiritual reading practice for today will, again, ask that you find a quiet place where you can comfortably read aloud. If possible, go to a location where you can close the door or be alone for a little while as you listen for God's word to you from 2 Timothy 3:14-17. Once you are settled in, turn to this passage. Before your read, take a deep breath and, releasing it, ask God to help you set aside any distractions for this time.

Now read aloud these four verses, reading slowly as though you are reading these words not only to yourself but also to others whom you love. Pause for a minute after the first reading, then read aloud again, listening for a word or phrase that catches your attention. Receive this one word or phrase, without analyzing or editing which word or phrase it may be. Take two or three minutes of silence to think about this word or phrase. What images come to mind with it? What feelings or emotions come to you as you silently repeat this word or phrase in your imagination, trusting that God has given it to you for some particular reason today? Take as much time as you want to explore where this word or phrase leads you. If you wish, take time to make notes or to journal.

Before you end your meditation time, read the verses aloud one final time, and as you do, offer these verses as a prayer for your faith community, for your family and friends, and for God's entire household. Place your prayer and life into God's hands, and receive God's prayer for you as you continue to live faithfully as a member of God's beloved family.

Group Meeting Experience

1 Thessalonians 1:2-10 | Thanksgiving

Imagine what it might be like if 1 Thessalonians were the only letter from Paul that you ever read. When the Thessalonians received this letter, they could not compare it to Paul's other letters nor to the Gospels because none of these had yet been written. In order to make sense of this letter, the Thessalonians had to draw on their prior experience of Paul, as well as on the content of the letter itself.

As noted in the general introduction to this episode, most people in the first century were unable to read and write. Letters like this one were read aloud to the gathered community. One of the first things those early hearers noticed was that the letter was written to the whole church as a community, and not to its individual members.

1. Like the other books of the New Testament, 1 Thessalonians was originally written in Greek, which distinguishes between singular and plural pronouns (that is, *you*, singular, looks very different from *you*, plural). Although it isn't obvious in the English translation, every time the word *you* appears in this letter, it refers to *you*, plural. Invite one person in your study group to read 1 Thessalonians 1:2-10 aloud, substituting the words *you all* each time he or she encounters the word *you*. (If you prefer, you may use whatever word or words indicate the plural *you* in your local dialect: *y'all, yous, you guys*, and so on.) What stands out for you as you hear all those *you all*'s in these opening verses? Are there images or phrases that you hear differently now as they emphasize the plural form of *you*? How do these verses speak to your church, faith community, or Bible study group as a whole?

2. Read through the "thanksgiving" passage (1 Thess 1:2-10) again, this time paying close attention to the details. What information do you learn about Paul? What do you learn about the Thessalonians? What do you learn about God, Jesus, and the Holy Spirit? Imagine that Paul is writing or speaking directly to you and your faith community: How do you see yourselves in this passage? How is the passage inviting all of you to grow or to change?

3. The "thanksgiving" passage functions like a preview of the whole letter, drawing attention to topics that will be addressed later. For example, notice the emphasis on activity that occurs in this passage. Look at the things that Paul and the community have done, how people act, and the impact of their behaviors on other people. (We see a similar emphasis on behavior and action in the other letters that we have read in the Covenant Bible Study.) The *work . . . effort . . .* and *perseverance* highlighted in 1 Thessalonians 1:3 comes from *faith . . . love . . .* and *hope*.

4. Compare our group study passage to 1 Thessalonians 3:6-13 and 4:9-11 (and if you have time, to 5:8-24). How do these passages pick up themes from 1 Thessalonians 1:2-10? Why does Paul place so much emphasis on the behavior of the community? What makes

it possible for the community to live in the ways that Paul commends? Is there a word or phrase from these passages that stands out for you? If so, how might you incorporate it into your life?

SIGNS OF FAITHFUL LOVE

Covenant people live responsible, changed lives at home and
in the community. Our lives display the same grace and goodness
toward others that we experience through God's love and faithfulness.

Wisdom: Proverbs and Ecclesiastes

DISCERNMENT
Finding what is good for my life

Bible Readings

Day 1: Proverbs 1–4

Day 2: Proverbs 10–15

Day 3: Proverbs 25–29

Day 4: Ecclesiastes 1–4

Day 5: Ecclesiastes 9–12

Day 6: Covenant Meditation on Ecclesiastes 3:1-8

Day 7: Group Meeting Experience with Proverbs 2:1-19

Covenant Prayer

For those of us blinded by greed, power, and selfish desires

You will understand the fear of the Lord, and discover the knowledge of God. (Proverbs 2:5)

For people trying to make sense of the world so they can live well in it

OUR LONGING FOR RELATIONSHIP

Wealth, knowledge, and power aren't satisfying. Our path to well-being is paved by God's wisdom.

Teach us to number our days so we can have a wise heart. (Psalm 90:12)

WISDOM LITERATURE

Ecclesiastes, the
Teacher, is described as
working hard to find
the wise word for his
community.

Proverbs, Ecclesiastes, and Job are the wisdom literature of ancient Israel. These books ponder in various ways the question: "What is good for my life?" They respond by drawing primarily from human experience, passing on the wisdom of elders and ancestors. They point to the natural world, confident that nature can teach us something about how to be wise as God's creatures; for example, "Go to the ant, you lazy person" (Prov 6:6). They also include and engage the wisdom of other cultures, such as Agur (Prov 30) and King Lemuel's mother (Prov 31:1-9), neither of whom are Israelites. In short, Israel's wisdom literature, which was part of a broader wisdom tradition in the ancient Near East, wrestles with how to live well in a world formed by God's wisdom.

The most celebrated wise person of ancient Israel is Solomon, the second and last king of the united monarchy (who probably lived from 966 to 926 BCE). Tradition tells us that Solomon's wisdom was granted by God, exceeded that of all others, and was celebrated by world leaders of his day (1 Kgs 3–11). Like David with the Psalms and Moses with the Torah (the Instruction), Solomon is identified with wisdom. Proverbs as a whole, or at least three of its sections, are attributed to him (Prov 1:1; 10:1; 25:1). So is the book of Ecclesiastes (Eccl 1:1). Although most interpreters think it is unlikely that Solomon wrote much, if any, of either book, his name gives significance and authority to both.

As the famous story of Solomon's judgment between two women quarreling over a baby suggests (1 Kgs 3:16-28), wisdom requires discernment. A wise person must be able to understand a situation and respond appropriately. It isn't enough to know traditions and texts. One must also know how to interpret contexts accurately. Notice how often Proverbs celebrates a word spoken at the right time. For example, "to give an appropriate answer is a joy; how good is a word at the right time!" (Prov 15:23). Other proverbs compare fitting speech to valuable and beautiful ornaments, such as gold apples in a silver setting (Prov 25:11) and gold earrings (Prov 25:12). The timely word is exquisite. Perhaps that is why Ecclesiastes, the Teacher, is described as working hard to find the wise word for his community. He listened and studied. He searched for "pleasing" words—speech that is at once appropriate and compelling. And he wrote "truthful words honestly" (Eccl 12:9-10). By contrast, fools are notorious for throwing words around, using proverbs willy-nilly. As a result, they harm others and themselves (Prov 26:7, 9). Fools don't take the time to understand the world around them.

PROVERBS

The wise know that every proverb is complex. A proverb is a brief statement of an apparent truth that is based on human experience and endures in a community over time. The term "proverb" is used for different forms of speech, from one-line sentences to longer poems. The most common form is the two-line proverb. The first line makes an observation or claim, which the second line develops, contrasts, or motivates. Other forms include "better than" proverbs (Eccl 7:1-3, 5, 8), numerical proverbs (Prov 30:18-19), "happy" proverbs (Prov 3:13; 28:14), commands (Prov 16:3), and prohibitions (Prov 22:22-23). Although proverbs are brief, they are packed with artistic insight. Proverbs often feature vivid images and play with words, sounds, or rhythms. And every proverb has more than one possible meaning. A proverb will convey a different meaning depending on who says it and how, to whom, or in what circumstances it is said. So discernment is required to use proverbs effectively.

The book of Proverbs contains some of Israel's wisdom as the community discerned and reinterpreted it over centuries, often at significant moments of building or rebuilding. The book is a collection of collections, nearly all of which have a separate title (for example, Prov 1:1; 10:1; 22:17). Proverbs 10–30 contains the oldest sections. They generally include oral folk proverbs that wise persons—sages who were associated with the royal court—gathered and edited. The process started perhaps as early as the time of Solomon (mid-tenth century BCE). Reference to "the men of Hezekiah, king of Judah" (Prov 25:1) suggests the work continued in the late eighth to early seventh centuries BCE, perhaps as part of Hezekiah's religious and political reforms. Finally, Proverbs 1–9 and 31:10-31 were added in the postexilic period (late sixth to early third centuries BCE). The assembling of the book thus began during the period of the monarchy, continued over generations, and drew to a close in the aftermath of the Babylonian exile as the community struggled to rebuild itself. Not surprisingly, the community in exile turned to age-old wisdom.

ECCLESIASTES

Ecclesiastes, whose name or title in Hebrew means "teacher" or "preacher," was a sage in Israel during the period after the exile (late sixth to third centuries BCE). The book recounts how he studied the world around him and tried to discern what is good for

Proverbs are complex. They are like all the fortune cookies of the community gathered together, their wisdom held in one place. Because proverbs have more than one meaning, discernment is required to know which life situations they fit best.

humans all of their days "under the sun" (Eccl 1:3). He judges much of what he sees to be pointless (Hebrew *hebel*), which in some contexts can mean "vapor" or "breath," or "that which can't be grasped." Indeed, he repeatedly observes that "everything is pointless, a chasing after wind" (Eccl 1:14; 2:26; 4:4). He points to such difficult realities as hard work and profits that don't satisfy (Eccl 5:10-17), injustices (Eccl 4:1-3; 5:8; 8:14), everyday hazards (Eccl 10:8-9), and the certainty and finality of death for everyone (Eccl 3:19-21). He describes how the world is turned upside down, with "slaves on horseback, while princes walk on foot like slaves" (Eccl 10:7). And he notes that even wisdom, which he still considers an advantage, can't guarantee success (Eccl 7:12). So what does Ecclesiastes conclude is good for the human? To seize and savor moments of joy—to eat and drink with a merry heart, to enjoy one's family and community, to find pleasure in one's labor (for example, Eccl 3:13; 5:18; 9:7-10). One must be quick to recognize and relish those moments as gifts from God.

Day 1: Proverbs 1–4
Learning discernment

The prologue to Proverbs (Prov 1:2-7) makes clear that the book's purpose is to teach wisdom. The prologue nearly bursts with vocabulary central to the work, such as *discipline*, *instruction*, *guidance*, *justice*, and *righteousness*. The terms are, on the one hand, clear and familiar. On the other hand, they name concepts that are complex and often contested. What is justice? What does righteousness look like? Whose discipline? Answering such questions in everyday circumstances requires discernment. Perhaps that is why the prologue insists that the book's audience is everyone—the young and the naive, the wise and those who understand (Prov 1:4-5). People never outgrow the need for instruction.

Set in a household in a city, Proverbs 1–9 contains the instructions of a father to his son(s). The setting is common in ancient Near Eastern wisdom literature. The father wants his children to choose the wise path, so he commends the teachings of parents and elders (Prov 1:8). He describes Wisdom as a woman who stands in the city and offers life-giving instruction (Prov 1:20-33). He urges the youth to search for wisdom as for "hidden treasure" (Prov 2:4) and declares that wisdom is a gift from God (Prov 2:6). The father also warns about the foolish path. He cautions about a street gang (Prov 1:10-19), wicked men (Prov 2:12-15; 4:14-19), and the "mysterious woman" (Prov 2:16-19), all of whom compete for the youth's attention. Pay attention to how the parent portrays the two paths and the consequences for choosing them.

How would you define some of the words that are central to Proverbs? What is discipline, instruction, guidance, justice, or righteousness? Can you imagine how someone else might define these words differently?

> **Optional:** *Additional videos on Woman Wisdom and the wise wife are available for download from* **CovenantBibleStudy.com**.

Day 2: Proverbs 10–15
Speaking the truth

The landscape changes significantly at Proverbs 10:1. Whereas Proverbs 1–9 contains long poetic instructions by a parent, Proverbs 10:1–22:16 consists primarily of two-line proverbs one after another. Each proverb stands on its own and seems, at least at first, disconnected from the proverbs around it. There is no apparent order. The arrangement can be disorienting.

Without the parent's guidance, readers now have responsibility for making sense of each proverb. We are invited to consider them slowly, one at a time, pondering whether we believe the proverb and imagining in what situations we might use it. We learn quickly that proverbs, like fine spices, have different senses; they "taste" different depending on the circumstances. So a wise person is careful about when and how she speaks. Notice how many proverbs in these chapters are about the power of speech. The wise word is honest (Prov 12:17) and life-giving (Prov 10:11, 17; 13:14; 14:25). It promotes peace (Prov 10:10; 15:1) and inspires joy (Prov 15:23). The foolish word, by contrast, harms oneself and others. Fools and the wicked lie, gossip, and stir up violence (Prov 10:6, 11; 11:9). Unlike the modern-day proverb that says, "Sticks and stones can break my bones, but words can never hurt me," the ancient sages recognized that speech can do real and significant damage.

When have you seen words do more damage than "sticks and stones"?

Day 3: Proverbs 25–29
Using power and influence wisely

Proverbs 25–29 focuses on the royal court and government. Indeed, some interpreters believe that portions of these chapters were used to prepare young men for leadership. The world that these proverbs describe appears more complicated than earlier in the book. We learn how to contend with kings, officials, bosses, enemies, gossips, sluggards, and liars. And for the first time, the sages warn about the precariousness of power. A morsel of bread buys injustice (Prov 28:21). Those who do right can be led astray (Prov 28:10). Wicked rulers trample the poor (Prov 28:15), steal from their people (Prov 29:4), and leave wrongdoings unpunished (Prov 29:16).

By this point in Proverbs, we are also aware that wisdom offers several perspectives on most topics. Skim through the book and identify proverbs that differ or even conflict about an issue. For example, some proverbs say that wealth is always good (Prov 10:15, 22; 14:20; 22:4). Others say it can be a liability (Prov 11:28). Some proverbs associate poverty with laziness (Prov 10:4; 24:33-34). Others point to violence and deceit (Prov 13:23; 21:6). The best example of different perspectives side by side is Proverbs 26:4-5: "Don't answer . . . Answer . . ." So what do we do? That requires discernment and paying close attention to one's particular situation. Both proverbs are wise in the right circumstances. See if you can list some modern-day proverbs that offer conflicting points of view, such as "Look before you leap" and "He who hesitates is lost"; or "Out of sight, out of mind" and "Absence makes the heart grow fonder."

When has someone passed on wisdom to you that helped you figure out a new situation (a new job, a new living situation, or a different culture or context)?

Day 4: Ecclesiastes 1–4
When life seems pointless

Ecclesiastes, the Teacher, wrote during a turbulent time in ancient Israel. In the Persian/early Hellenistic period (late sixth to third centuries BCE), the economy became increasingly commercialized and competitive, and taxes and interest rates were high. The result was a very slippery socioeconomic ladder. Some people got ahead quickly. Others lost everything overnight (Eccl 5:13-16). There were no guarantees that hard work would produce security. That reality prompts Ecclesiastes' central question: "What do people gain from all the hard work that they work so hard at under the sun?" (Eccl 1:3).

The Teacher responds that "everything is pointless" (*hebel*, or "vapor"; Eccl 1:2). It can't be grasped. It is pointless. He comes to that conclusion by discernment. He looks at the world around him and reflects on what he sees. Notice how often the phrases "I said to myself," "I applied my mind," "I saw," and "I observed" repeat in these chapters. What Ecclesiastes sees is a weary, repetitive world: generations come and go; the sun rises and sets; the winds blow round and round (Eccl 1:3-11). There is constant activity but "nothing new" (Eccl 1:9). Ecclesiastes doesn't see progress or a grand design. Yet humans keep chasing "after wind" (Eccl 1:14; 2:11, 17, 26). They work tirelessly to try to secure their happiness. Ecclesiastes does, too (Eccl 2:1-11). But what the Teacher discovers is that none of it is certain or permanent. Bad and unexpected things happen, and death comes for everyone.

The humble and wise person sees a world that doesn't make sense, where the rules don't work the way they should, and where there are no guarantees. Everyone dies, so living wisely is about finding the moments of joy one has: family, friends, simple meals, and good work done well. Do you make time for this kind of wisdom in your own life?

> **Optional:** *An additional video on the different kinds of proverbs is available for download from* **CovenantBibleStudy.com**.

Day 5: Ecclesiastes 9–12
Everyday moments of joy

Ecclesiastes' observations of the world could leave him in despair. But instead he looks around for signs of hope. Ecclesiastes takes all of his observations to heart (Eccl 9:1) and shares what he can say with certainty about the world. Although death comes for everyone, it is better to live than to die (Eccl 9:4-6). Because time and chance happen to everyone, it is better to eat, drink, enjoy life with those whom you love, and do your work with all your might (Eccl 9:7-10). And while weapons might be powerful, wisdom is still an advantage. It can save a city (Eccl 9:13-18; 10:10). Ecclesiastes studies the world around him and concludes that the "word of truth" his community needs to hear is a call to relish everyday moments of joy (Eccl 8:15-16; 12:9-10).

Ecclesiastes is one of several voices in Israelite wisdom literature that emphasize the limits of human knowledge. Notice how often he asks "Who knows?" and declares that "No one knows" or "You don't know." Consider how frequently he speaks in relative terms, such as "This is better than that." Ecclesiastes recognizes that human understanding only goes so far. Ultimately, it bumps into the mystery of God, whose works and purposes are unknowable despite a sense of "eternity" that God placed in the human heart (Eccl 3:11; 11:5). To claim to know more than we do is simply hubris and folly.

Think of someone in your life who is unafraid to say "I don't know." Why is that difficult for so many? Can it be liberating?

Day 6: Ecclesiastes 3:1-8
Covenant Meditation: What is good for my life?

Today's reading will be Ecclesiastes 3:1-8. For many people in the church, the words of these eight verses of scripture are well known, for they are frequently read at funerals and memorial services. In fact, in the Christian tradition, wisdom literature is commonly placed in services of remembrance. In these times of communal memory, grief, and honor, a proverb or a line of poetry can do in short, clear measure what might otherwise take a paragraph's worth of fresh words.

Our spiritual reading practice will be anchored in the question: "What is good for my life?" Our author for this week's Bible study suggests the wisdom books, including Ecclesiastes, all ponder this question in various ways. Allowing a single question to frame our reading of a passage can help form us in the spiritual practice of discernment, that is, of learning to search out and listen for God's voice, light, and direction in the midst of everyday life's layers and noise. To ask God, "What is good for my life?" while turning to a time-honored scripture, and then to let the scripture prompt stories, people, images, hope, and prayers—trusting that what comes to mind is also on God's heart—is one way to begin to allow scripture to teach us discernment.

For today's practice, begin by reading silently through the eight verses once, just to observe each carefully selected word and phrase. Then, before your second reading, ask God in prayer: "What is good for my life?" Then read each verse one at a time, resting for a few moments at the end of each verse and staying with any thoughts about people, circumstances, emotions, longings, worries, or desires that come to mind for you out of the verse. It may be helpful to pray the question again between each verse: "God, what is good for my life?" Go slowly and try to really trust that what comes to mind, even if it doesn't seem to make sense in the moment, is something between you and God, something that leads toward goodness for your life.

When you have prayed for discernment through all eight verses, offer a silent prayer to God of thanksgiving and for clarity for your life. Close with "Amen."

Group Meeting Experience

Proverbs 2:1-19 | *How to become wise*

In Proverbs 2, the parent encourages the youth to search for wisdom. The chapter is one long speech of twenty-two verse units, the number of consonants in the Hebrew alphabet. The effect is a sense of completeness: This is the description of how one becomes wise. It is a collaborative effort between parents, the youth, and God. By describing the path to discernment for the young, the sage describes the path to discernment for all God's people.

1. Outline the main units of Proverbs 2:1-22. Pay attention to the use of the word *then* to signal the results of the search for wisdom. Look also for repeated images and phrases. How does the parent build his case? What steps does he identify in the quest for wisdom?

2. The parent insists that the youth must actively seek wisdom. What exactly does the youth need to do? What does that suggest about how a person learns?

3. How does a person finally gain wisdom? What is significant about gaining it?

4. Circle the terms the parent uses for wisdom. What exactly do the wise understand? What happens when God gives someone wisdom and discernment?

5. The parent says that the youth will understand "fear of the LORD" (Prov 2:5). "Fear of the LORD" is the refrain of Proverbs. It frames Proverbs 1–9 (Prov 1:7; 9:10) and the book as a whole (Prov 31:30), and it is found frequently throughout. Indeed, the aim of the book is arguably to form "fearers of the LORD," that is, people who revere God, recognize their capacities and limitations, and work for good with insight, energy, and humility (Prov 3:5-8; 15:33). How is the concept of "fear of the LORD," reverence for God, similar to or different from the ways you think about wisdom?

6. How does the parent depict threats to wisdom? What is helpful and problematic about a parent's warnings? Compare the mysterious woman in this chapter with the wise woman in Proverbs 1.

7. How do we encourage the search for wisdom and true discernment today? Would you identify the same steps to wisdom as the parent does in Proverbs 2? Why or why not?

SIGNS OF FAITHFUL LOVE

Covenant people search for wisdom. In the pursuit of wisdom,
we experience well-being and everyday moments of joy.

Philemon, Philippians, Colossians, Ephesians

RECONCILED
Repairing broken relationships

Bible Readings

Day 1: Philemon

Day 2: Philippians 1–4

Day 3: Colossians 1:1–3:17

Day 4: Ephesians 1:1–5:20

Day 5: Colossians 3:18–4:1; Ephesians 5:21–6:9

Day 6: Covenant Meditation on Philemon 1:4-7

Day 7: Group Meeting Experience with Ephesians 2

Covenant Prayer

Thank you, merciful God.

He brought us to life with Christ while we were dead. (Ephesians 2:4)

We are created in Christ Jesus to do good things.

God planned for these good things to be the way that we live our lives. (Ephesians 2:10)

OUR LONGING FOR RELATIONSHIP

We each have flaws in our relationships that pull us apart in our homes and within the body of Christ.

PRISON LETTERS

Paul's Prison Letters give readers a glimpse into some of his closest relationships and his biggest ideas about God's secret plan to bring reconciliation through Jesus Christ. Just as these letters are written "in prison," they also engage what it means to live "in Christ." The theme of knowledge also permeates these letters and is linked to the experience of living "in Christ."

PHILEMON

The shortest and most personal of Paul's letters, Philemon was written from prison (either in Ephesus, Caesarea, or Rome). It's addressed to an individual first and only then to "the church that meets in your house" (Phlm 1:2). Philemon is a wealthy leader in one of Paul's congregations. He probably owned many slaves, perhaps twenty to thirty, if his household was like most large households of the day. Philemon and the congregation are probably located in Colossae, providing a connection between this letter and another we will discuss (compare Col 1:7; 4:10-14; Phlm 1:23).

Paul's purpose in writing this letter is a matter of debate. The most common suggestion is that Paul wanted Philemon to accept his slave Onesimus back without punishment. Runaway slaves were often subjected to severe punishment once recaptured. One common form of punishment was branding the letter *F* (for "fugitive") on a prominent part of the slave's body. So Paul wants Philemon to subdue his potential anger. The alternative suggestion is that Paul was asking Philemon indirectly to free Onesimus so that he could join Paul's missionary team. Paul's letter is crafty and peppered with humor, puns, irony, and double meanings. Philemon, like us, probably read the letter several times to figure out what Paul wanted.

PHILIPPIANS

Again we find Paul imprisoned, although we aren't sure where (Ephesus, Caesarea, or Rome). The congregation sent Epaphroditus to minister to Paul's needs while he was in prison (Phil 2:25, 30). Unlike modern prisons, inmates were dependent upon others for food, clothing, and other needs. This extraordinary effort of the Philippians, to provide for Paul's repeated financial support

(Phil 4:10-20) while he was incarcerated, points to the special relationship that existed between the apostle and this congregation.

Paul has opponents in Philippi. His description of these adversaries is general, so we can't be certain of their identity. They urged circumcision. They also seem allergic to self-denial (Phil 3:19). They appear to focus more on Christ's resurrection than his crucifixion. They apparently even believed that they were perfect. This would account for Paul's denial of his own perfection (Phil 3:12) and for his emphasis on the cross of Christ (Phil 3:8-11). Finally, given Paul's emphasis on his own Jewish identity (Phil 3:5-6) and their emphasis on circumcision, they were probably also Christian Jews.

In addition to this problem with opponents, Paul is also concerned with divisions in the fellowship. Near the letter's end, Paul calls upon two women, Euodia and Syntyche, "to come to an agreement in the Lord" (Phil 4:2). Clearly they are so significant to the leadership of this church that their disagreement matters greatly. These women "have struggled together with [Paul] in the ministry of the gospel, along with Clement and the rest of [Paul's] coworkers whose names are in the scroll of life" (Phil 4:3). If we think Paul insisted that people agree with him on all matters, it may be because his letters usually address problems he considers central to the gospel. Disputes like these demonstrate that in other matters, the apostle recognized that differences were inevitable and that a spirit of reconciliation should prevail.

COLOSSIANS

We do a "double take" when reading Colossians in light of the other letters of Paul. The apostle is credited as the author, but the literary expression seems different, and most interpreters think that Colossians and Ephesians were written by a faithful disciple of Paul in his name. We encounter in this letter several new phrases that are peculiar because of their absence from other Pauline letters. In addition to the new phrases, there is the provocative statement: "I'm completing what is missing from Christ's sufferings with my own body. I'm doing this for the sake of his body, which is the church" (Col 1:24). This language goes well beyond other statements made by Paul where he relates his own suffering to that of Christ.

On the other hand, Colossians' close ties with Philemon seem to suggest that Paul wrote it himself (for example, both send greetings from Aristarchus, Mark, Epaphras, Luke, and Demas; both

Paul, in chains, pleads with Philemon on behalf of the runaway slave Onesimus to be reconciled with him as a brother in Christ.

For a complete chart of Paul's ministry and writing, see the CEB Study Bible, *NT page 244.*

Unlike modern prisons, inmates were dependent upon others for food, clothing, and other needs.

call Archippus a minister; and both mention Onesimus). The congregation was founded by Epaphras in a place where Paul was unknown (Col 2:1). He did this as Paul's deputy (Col 1:7). The purpose of Colossians seems to be a report on the apostle's situation in prison, which would be described more fully by Tychicus, who was most likely carrying the letter (Col 4:8). In the process a vague warning is given to the members of the fellowship (Col 2:8-23). It isn't clear whether the dangers stem from within or from outside the Colossian church.

One of the most defining features of Colossians is its cosmic scope. Elsewhere, Paul cites traditions presenting Christ as preexistent (Phil 2:6-11) and as God's agent in creation (1 Cor 8:6). He also envisions the cosmic redemption of all creation (Rom 8:18-25). In Colossians, however, we encounter a Christ who transcends human boundaries of time and space. He plays an expanded role in creation, and his work of redemption stretches across time. Christ is at the highest level of the cosmic order: "All the treasures of wisdom and knowledge are hidden in him" (Col 2:3). He is God's "secret plan" (or "mystery"; Col 2:2). We as believers are encouraged to delve into this secret plan in order to experience fully the reconciliation that Christ accomplished so that we can be presented to God "as a people who are holy, faultless, and without blame" (Col 1:22).

EPHESIANS

Most interpreters consider Ephesians to be an expansion of Colossians. The words "in Ephesus" are actually missing from the oldest manuscripts, and a convincing argument can be made that this isn't a letter but an encyclical, which is a sermon meant to be shared by many churches. Ephesians has gifted the church with many beautiful themes and memorable passages, including: the lofty potential of the church; the unity of believers across polity, race, and ethnic identity (Eph 3:15); donning the armor of God against destructive powers; and the stunning benediction in Ephesians 3:20-21. Like Colossians, Ephesians has also raised ethical concerns from some modern Christians due to its acceptance of destructive hierarchical relationships, including approval of human slavery (Eph 6:5). It is ironic that just a few verses later the author calls us to resist powers and principalities, not to mention the earlier insistence that Christ has broken down "the barrier of hatred that divided us" (Eph 2:14).

Day 1: Philemon

Reconciliation of "brothers"

Philemon is unlike other Pauline letters. It avoids theological language in tone and argument. The letter mentions God only twice. Here Paul isn't thinking through the meaning and implications of the death and resurrection of Jesus Christ—if we read this letter quickly. If, however, we read it slowly and deliberately, then we experience a conversation arising from lived theology.

The key to unlocking the theology of Paul's argument is the phrase "in Christ." The number of times Paul refers to Christ in this letter stands out in itself—11 times in 25 verses. Paul speaks of himself as being "a prisoner for the cause of Christ Jesus" (Phlm 1). His boldness toward Philemon has to do with the slave owner's faith in Christ. Paul's order or command rests on how deeply they both are immersed in this "partnership" that characterizes life in Christ. Now that Onesimus has joined this partnership, Paul's main concern is to bring about reconciliation between alienated "brothers," individuals of equal status in the eyes of the Lord. This type of behavior, from Paul's perspective, was as essential to his ministry as preaching the gospel in the first place (see, for example, 2 Cor 5:18-20).

Are you estranged from someone, such as a relative or a friend or a coworker? Even if it seems too late, imagine what reconciliation would look like. How would forgiveness feel?

Day 2: Philippians 1–4

Reconciliation and the fellowship of believers

Like Philemon, the Philippians are Paul's "partners in the ministry of the gospel" (Phil 1:5). So close is the bond between the church and its founder that some have seen this as a friendship letter, a well-defined literary type within the ancient world. Several of the features that typified such letters occur in Philippians: a strong sense of partnership (Phil 1:7); his longing for them (Phil 1:8; 4:1); shared experiences (Phil 1:30); affectionate language

(Phil 4:1); sharing gifts (Phil 4:10-20); and familial forms of address (Phil 1:12, 14; 3:1, 13, 17; 4:1, 8).

One of the dominant ideas in this letter is that of "knowing" (Phil 3:8). Paul's language suggests a kind of knowledge that is different from the mastery of doctrine and more than self-awareness. It is a way of knowing that transforms us even as it reveals who we are. It is the kind of knowledge that makes us transparent before Christ. In fact, it forms the core of our new understanding of ourselves. In one sense, the relationship created is one of spiritual union—being "found in him" (Phil 3:9). In another sense, the relationship created promotes a lens through which we navigate the world— "the participation in his sufferings" and "being conformed to his death" (Phil 3:10). This kind of knowing emphasizes binding together individuals in the fellowship, and binding the fellowship to Christ.

Imagine a close friend. Do you talk often? Are you honest and transparent with each other? Do you suffer when your friend suffers? Do you know Jesus as a friend like this?

Day 3: Colossians 1:1–3:17
Reconciliation as the hidden treasure of God

We can locate this book's purpose in Colossians 2:2-3. This passage identifies a core feature of the letter: At the heart of the faith is the hidden treasure of God's secret plan, whose content is Christ himself. This language suggests that there are many ways of probing, many ways of knowing. Framed in this manner, the secret plan that ends in Christ begins with God.

As in Philippians, reconciliation and knowing are intertwined in Colossians. The letter gives depth to God's character. Although the author says that God is "invisible," God is never entirely out of the picture. The challenge isn't to keep God in mind, as though knowing God were a matter of concentrating solely on God. Knowing God's will is a God-given capacity that comes in response to answered prayer. It is a special gift of discernment (Col 1:9). While this kind of knowledge may be experienced in a flash of insight, it is a knowledge that grows over time (Col 1:10). It may even take a lifetime. While Philippians focuses on Christ giving up the "form of God," Colossians focuses on the cross as the sacrificial death through which God achieved universal reconciliation (Col 1:19-20, 22).

Try to put God's secret plan in your own words. What did Jesus accomplish on the cross?

Day 4: Ephesians 1:1–5:20
Reconciliation as the cosmic reality

When the author uses the word *church*, he normally has a local congregation in mind (for example, Corinth, Philippi, Colossae). Ephesians, by contrast, focuses exclusively on the universal church. In Colossians, the universal church is also emphasized, but the local congregation is sometimes the point of reference (see Col 4:15-16). This difference of perspective helps explain why Paul in his other letters envisions ministries as gifts that are exercised primarily in local churches (compare 1 Cor 12:4-11; Rom 12:3-8). Similarly, duly appointed leadership roles are based in a congregation (for example, Phil 1:1). By reflecting a more comprehensive perspective, Ephesians sees the universal church as built upon a foundation of "apostles and prophets"—an earlier generation—with Christ as the cornerstone (Eph 2:20).

Ephesians also displays considerable creativity with metaphors for the church. Like Colossians, it understands "the body of Christ" to be the universal church (Eph 4:12-13). Christ, as cosmic ruler, is the head of the church, "God's household" where Christians work out the implications of their faith. The most innovative metaphor, however, is the church as the "one new person" formed from the fusion of Jews and Gentiles who are reconciled by the death of Jesus Christ (Eph 2:15-16).

Think of something that divides the church, God's household. Do we still divide over race? Are there other dividing lines that we establish but that the cross makes untenable?

Day 5: Colossians 3:18–4:1; Ephesians 5:21–6:9

A reconciled household

Christ's exaltation in Colossians and Ephesians creates its own form of obedient submission. We as the church (the body of Christ) are subordinate to our head, which is Christ himself. An appropriate posture then emerges. We are to "submit to each other out of respect for Christ" (Eph 5:21), and the church itself lives in submission to Christ (Eph 5:24). Recognizing Christ as head means yielding to Christ's supreme authority. The body metaphor suggests that growth is the maturation that the church experiences over time.

The image of the body of Christ points to a covenant community that stresses unity, mutual commitment, and reconciliation. Note how Christ and the church are imagined in terms of a wife's and a husband's responsibilities. Relationships here are structured hierarchically—wives, children, and slaves are expected to be subordinate and obedient—but these expectations are cast in terms of mutual respect and love (Eph 5:21). Many Christians would argue that hierarchy and equality are in practice mutually exclusive. In the author's own time, the household was structured as a miniature version of the government. Envision a pyramid with the emperor at the top, then the aristocracy, then down to the widest part of the pyramid on the bottom: slaves and other vulnerable populations. One-third of all people in the Roman Empire were slaves.

Should Christian households be organized as miniature versions of the nation or state, or should another structure pertain? What family structure do you think best reflects Christian principles? How does Christ's journey to the cross inform your view of God's household?

Day 6: Philemon 1:4-7
Covenant Meditation: Reconciled in Christ

Our reading on Day 1 this week encourages us not to overlook the "lived theology" of Paul's letter to Philemon. But now we will slow down and reread this text. We will, through prayer, revisit this faithful word between brothers who don't agree but are united by Christ through love.

Begin by turning to Philemon 1:4-7. This is "Paul's prayer for Philemon." Slowly read this text. Now recall someone in your life—perhaps a family member, work colleague, teacher, friend, or acquaintance—for whom you can offer this same prayer. It may be someone with whom you have a difference of opinion or some obstacle in your relationship, or it could be someone who isn't in disagreement with you. It simply should be someone for whom you give God thanks, who shares your faith in Christ, and who serves God and the faith community in a way that you have noticed but perhaps not affirmed before.

Place this person's name at the beginning of this prayer, and offer this prayer for him or her. As you pray, hold this person in your imagination and in God's life-giving light. Throughout the day, lift your brother or sister in prayer whenever possible. At the end of the day, give God thanks for this scripture and this person.

Group Meeting Experience
Ephesians 2 | From death to reconciled life

Our study of these Prison Letters comes near the middle of Covenant Bible Study. In particular, these letters focus on the core challenge of covenant life: being reconciled with God and with God's household. To bring this theme to mind, we started with a concrete instance of reconciliation (Philemon) and moved to the cosmic need for reconciliation (Ephesians).

Ephesians begins with an extended opening (Eph 1:1-23). It ends with a grandiose statement about the cosmic Christ: "God put everything under Christ's feet and made him head of everything in the church, which is his body. His body, the church, is the fullness of Christ, who fills everything in every way" (Eph 1:22-23). This statement sets the stage for all that follows in the letter.

1. Our reading opens with a depiction of our former reality and conduct (Eph 2:1-3). Why were we "at one time" like dead people? What does the author mean when he says, "You followed the rule of a destructive spiritual power" (Eph 2:2)? Is there any suggestion as to who or what this destructive spiritual power is?

2. Ephesians 2:4-7 presents God's act of intervention and the reconciliation it brought. What motivated God's act of intervention? What does it mean that God didn't act because of our lovable behavior but out of a wealth of divine mercy and an abundance of love? "You are saved by God's grace because of your faith," says the apostle (Eph 2:8). How do these verses remind us of the "before" and "after" of salvation? Does this act of grace make our own actions irrelevant, or does it set up an expectation?

3. Ephesians 2:8 serves as a foundation for the popular personal proclamation "I am saved." How is this different from what Paul says in Philippians 2:12-13? How are we to understand or interpret the differences?

4. Ephesians 2:11-22 uses the images of "aliens," "citizens," and "strangers" alongside the religious and ethnic division of Jews and Gentiles. How are these ideas related to "the covenants of God's promise" (Eph 2:12) and those who lack such access? What does it mean that Christ broke down the barrier (Eph 2:14)?

5. Ephesians 2:19-22 proclaims that Gentiles are "no longer strangers and aliens" but are members of "God's household." How does the foundation described in Ephesians 2:20 differ from what we find in Matthew 16:18? What role does Christ as the cornerstone play in this image of the church? How can the church exemplify the barrier-free life discussed here?

SIGNS OF FAITHFUL LOVE

Covenant people know the secret plan of living in Christ,
who reconciles us to God and others, by living life each
day with mutual respect and an abundance of love.

James, Jude, 1 and 2 Peter

ACT LIKE A CHRISTIAN
Practicing what we believe

Bible Readings

Day 1: James 1–2

Day 2: James 3–5

Day 3: 1 Peter 1:3–4:11

Day 4: 1 Peter 4:12–5:14

Day 5: Jude and 2 Peter

Day 6: Covenant Meditation on James 1:22-26

Day 7: Group Meeting Experience with 1 Peter 2:4-10

Covenant Prayer

For all who have been bullied, teased, or ridiculed

I take refuge in you, Lord, my God. Save me from all who chase me! Rescue me! (Psalm 7:1)

For those who stand up to bullies and become a friend to those who are despised

My brothers and sisters, what good is it if people say they have faith but do nothing to show it? (James 2:14)

OUR LONGING FOR RELATIONSHIP

As Christians, we sometimes speak harshly to each other and to others who are watching to see if we practice what we preach.

JAMES, JUDE, 1 AND 2 PETER

Each of these four books was written to provide guidance to Christians living toward the end of the first century CE. Each is full of advice for faithful covenant living in light of an unbelieving and sometimes even hostile community outside the church. Each was probably written pseudonymously—that is, a faithful early Christian writer sought to gain authority and credibility for his work by writing in the name of a Christian from an earlier era.

Peter was of course one of the most prominent of Jesus' disciples. He is mentioned in every Gospel and also in the writings of Paul (1 Cor 9; Gal 2). Peter is a nickname meaning "rock" that Jesus gave to his disciple Simon, who, along with his brother Andrew, left the family fishing business to become a disciple. It's no wonder that Christians writing toward the end of the first century would choose to honor Peter by naming their books after him.

Jesus had brothers named James and Jude. It seems likely that the authors of the letters by those names claimed that they stood in such a close relationship to Jesus' own teaching that they could name his brothers as authorities for what they wrote.

It's also striking that both James and 1 Peter read more like speeches or sermons than like conversational letters. They have the beginning salutations that we expect from a letter (compare the letters of Paul, such as 1 Corinthians or Galatians). James, however, lacks the usual farewell greeting of a first-century letter.

Second Peter and Jude were probably written later than James and 1 Peter. Both deal with the particular problem of how to live faithfully when the end of time seems to be delayed almost indefinitely. First Peter is written with the expectation that the end is near. Second Peter is written in realization that this final act isn't coming as soon as Christians had thought. Second Peter and Jude contain much of the same material; one author almost certainly copied from the other.

JAMES

The letter from James is full of good advice for Christian living. It's much like the book of Proverbs in its trust that human wisdom, can understand God's wisdom, and that if we live by that wisdom, we will be faithful to God's covenant with us. "Are any of you wise and understanding? Show that your actions are good with a humble lifestyle that comes from wisdom" (Jas 3:13).

James makes two points with special power. First, James disagrees with those who misinterpret Paul's stress on faith and who think that Paul claims it doesn't matter what you do. James reminds us how important it is to practice what we believe, to act out our convictions: "As the lifeless body is dead, so faith without actions is dead" (Jas 2:26).

> **Optional:** *An additional video on James and Paul is available for download from* **CovenantBibleStudy.com**.

Second, James is concerned that the churches he knows are showing favoritism toward people who are rich and are neglecting the needs of those who are poor. He wants to make sure that powerless people are treated with just as much hospitality as the powerful. Indeed, he shows a profound suspicion of the rich and powerful (see Jas 5:1-6).

Like the book of Proverbs, the letter of James is full of lively pictures that the author uses to make his point. "Think about this: a small flame can set a whole forest on fire. The tongue is a small flame of fire, a world of evil at work in us" (Jas 3:5-6).

> **Optional:** *An additional video on how the book of James speaks about the tongue is available for download from* **CovenantBibleStudy.com**.

If we had only James to read in the New Testament, we wouldn't know nearly enough of the abundant mercy of God in Jesus Christ. If we got rid of James, we wouldn't think hard enough about how to serve that mercy in our relationships with others.

1 PETER

First Peter is a letter written to seven churches in Asia Minor. The order in which the churches are listed in 1 Peter 1:1 may suggest the route that the letter took as it was carried from church to church.

The letter can be divided into two sections: 1 Peter 1:1–4:11 and 1 Peter 4:12–5:11. The first section deals with the theme of the new life that God gives to believers. The stress on new birth is so strong

If we live by God's wisdom, we will be faithful to God's covenant.

77

The early readers of
1 Peter faced pressure
to return to the
comfortable ways of
their culture's popular
religions. Peter
wants them to know
that if they do this,
they misunderstand
their own identity as
covenant people.

that some have thought that this section of the letter was originally a baptismal sermon. The second part of the letter deals more
directly with the threat of harassment and gives advice to Christians in distress. Both sections recognize that the churches are facing some kind of trial.

We have no idea whether the harassment of which 1 Peter writes
included physical punishment or even martyrdom. It almost certainly
included being shunned and derided by the majority of the people in
their towns.

First Peter is written for people who are called immigrants and
strangers (see 1 Pet 1:17-18 and 2:11-12). Here the letter may be refer-
ring to their actual legal status as persons who arrived from another
country, or it may be that these Christians are exiles from their heavenly
home. Either way, it's also clear that these Christians feel like immigrants
because they have been cut off from the pagan communities and practices where they have been at home.

Strikingly, without explanation or apology, 1 Peter simply takes terms
that the Old Testament applies to Israel and applies them to the first-
century church.

The whole letter is shaped by the firm conviction that at the end of
time God will judge all people fairly and bring history to its consummation. This letter is written to tell Christians how to live in the meantime.

2 PETER AND JUDE

Jude and 2 Peter are probably the last two books to be written in
the Bible. Both are concerned with theological inaccuracies and moral
failings among self-designated believers. Second Peter, the more thorough letter, apparently knows and uses Jude. The author establishes his
authority by claiming (as Peter) to have been present at Jesus' transfigu-
ration. He addresses the problem of Jesus' delayed return by insisting
first that God's mathematics aren't like our own and by suggesting that
the delay in Jesus' return allows time for people to change their hearts
and lives.

These formerly pagan
Christians aren't just
"like" Israel. In the new
era of Jesus Christ,
they are Israel.

Day 1: James 1–2
Faith and impartiality

In these chapters, the author warns his readers against two mistakes that are easy for Christians to make. The first mistake results from paying attention too closely to the standards of the world. The second mistake results from misreading one of the great sources of the church—Paul's letters.

James notices that it is too easy for church members to apply the standards of the world to the community of faith. If people have prestige in the larger world, it is easy to give them special prestige in the church. If people are wealthy, it is easy to prefer them over the poor (see Jas 1:9-12 and 2:1-7).

James insists on the centrality of faith for Christian life and community. Faith is a great gift from God. It is tested and refined in difficult times. It is contrasted above all to doubt. Faithful people are single-minded; doubtful people wander and waffle (Jas 1:2-7).

However, James fears that his hearers misunderstand the nature of faith. Either James and his congregation know some of the writings of the apostle Paul, or they have a sense of the kind of gospel that is being preached in Paul's name. James claims that the Christian life always has two movements. First is the movement of belief, and second is the movement of charity and compassion on the part of the faithful. The charity is evidence of the faith (Jas 2:14-26).

Think of examples in your life where your faithfulness or trust in God is evident in your actions.

Day 2: James 3–5
Penitence and patience

Like the book of Proverbs in the Old Testament, James presents a series of wise sayings to help Christians conduct their lives. Like Proverbs, James believes that such human wisdom is a reflection of the divine wisdom that is a gift from God (Jas 3:13-18).

When this letter calls us to wisdom, it calls us to pay close attention to the way the world really goes. A careful look will reveal that in the world—and in the church—the tongue has considerable power to bless, to curse, and to slander. The wise Christian will use the tongue wisely (Jas 3:1-12). In the world—and in the church—jealousy and envy are frequently the cause of strife and even warfare (Jas 3:13-14; 4:1-3).

Because all of us stand in need of heavenly wisdom and fall short of that wisdom, we all are called to change our hearts and lives before a just and merciful God (Jas 4:4-10). James continues to affirm his concern for impartiality by suggesting that the wealthy, who have more goods, will have more need to change their lives (Jas 5:1-6).

The fruit of a changed life is patience. Trusting in the mercy of God, faithful Christians wait for the fulfillment of divine wisdom in God's providential time (Jas 5:7-11).

Reflect on whether you use your tongue wisely. If you are frequently impatient, what needs to change about your relationship with God and with others?

Day 3: 1 Peter 1:3–4:11
New life guided by Christ

These verses are rich in their assertion that lives guided by Christ require and provide a new beginning for our old lives: "Don't be conformed to your former desires, those that shaped you when you were ignorant. But, as obedient children, you must be holy in every aspect of your lives" (1 Pet 1:14-15; see 1 Pet 4:1-6).

When Peter tells the believers that they are "immigrants and strangers in the world" (1 Pet 2:11), he emphasizes that they are now separated from their former way of life and are called to live by new standards of faithfulness and obedience while they await Christ's coming.

It is striking, however, that the new life Peter envisions doesn't really include new social structures. Rather, he suggests that Christians live in the present social structures in ways that are relatively charitable and kind. This becomes a problem when he simply assumes a hierarchical view of the family and tells slaves to bear cruelty patiently.

Yet over against this support for the social status quo, there is a reminder that, read through the ages, suggests a more radical reordering of life in Christ: "Finally, all of you be of one mind, sympathetic, lovers of your fellow believers, compassionate, and modest in your opinion of yourselves. Don't pay back evil for evil or insult for insult. Instead, give blessing in return" (1 Pet 3:8-9).

If someone at school, at work, or in the community suspected you were a Christian, what kind of clues would they gather from watching your life?

Day 4: 1 Peter 4:12–5:14
Waiting for the last days

The New Testament assumes that the future of history is in God's hands and that God will bring history to its conclusion. Moreover, the New Testament claims that the conclusion of human history will be generous, merciful, and just.

First Peter is written for Christians in Asia Minor who are suffering some kind of distress. We have no idea whether there was a general harassment of Christians, or whether a smaller number of Christians were suffering at the hands of the authorities, or whether they were suffering the distance and exclusion from their former pagan friends. It's clear, though, that Christians are to live humbly and faithfully in light of the coming fulfillment of history. Part of that humble living will require a church as orderly as the households Peter admires. Elders—probably both in age and in office—will rule kindly; younger members—probably both in age and in faith—will obey (1 Pet 5:1-5). It's also clear that fulfillment will be God's fulfillment, and full of grace. "After you have suffered for a little while, the God of all grace, the one who called you into his eternal glory in Christ Jesus, will himself restore, empower, strengthen, and establish you" (1 Pet 5:10; see 1 Pet 4:12-19).

Think about whether painful experiences or personal suffering has strengthened your faithfulness.

Day 5: Jude and 2 Peter

When the great day is delayed

The letter from Jude is especially concerned with false teaching and false behavior. In such literature, the opponents are almost always characterized harshly as being wrong intellectually and being inexcusable morally. While it is almost impossible to sort out just what Jude opposes, it's clear what the letter affirms: "Keep each other in the love of God, wait for the mercy of our Lord Jesus Christ, who will give you eternal life" (Jude 1:21).

Second Peter picks up much of the same concern for those who are led astray, but holds fast the hope in God's consummation of history while dealing with a problem: Why is this consummation taking so long? The answer is twofold. First, God's time isn't our time, so we shouldn't put confidence in our own highly speculative timetables. Second, the delay is God's gracious way of allowing time for changed hearts and the conversion of unbelievers.

As with 1 Peter and Jude, the time of waiting is also to be a time of obedience and faithfulness—and hope. The final verse of 2 Peter isn't just a formula; it's an admonition and a promise: "Grow in the grace and knowledge of our Lord and savior Jesus Christ. To him belongs glory now and forever" (2 Pet 3:18).

How do you typically deal with delay when systems or serious flaws are changing slowly? Are you patient? Do you look for greener pastures? Are you an activist who tries to make something happen?

Day 6: James 1:22-26

Covenant Meditation: Doers of the word

Through this week's readings, we studied biblical texts in which the authors offered early Christians guidance for faithful living, especially in difficult or hostile environments. It's just as true today that following the way of Jesus isn't easy. Our choices, behaviors, and responses to daily circumstances must be made in a context where our faith in Christ continues to be countercultural. To follow Christ requires intention, discernment, and practice. With this week's theme, "Act Like a Christian," our spiritual practice invites us to reflect on Christian behavior through prayer.

First, find a space that is as quiet as possible—a place with no interruptions (from phone, computer, coworkers, others). All you need is your source of scripture and the time you can give to this practice (ten to fifteen minutes is adequate). Sit in a comfortable position. Locate James 1:22-26 and mark its place for easy return.

Before you begin to read, relax your breath and body, setting aside as many distractions as possible—task lists, appointments, unfinished conversations. Try to imagine giving these distractions to God for a while. They will wait for you until you complete this time of prayer.

Now read James 1:22-26 aloud, softly, and slowly. When you are finished, take a deep breath in and out. Then read the passage again, reflecting on each word and phrase as you read. At the end of this second reading, return to a word, phrase, or verse that catches your attention for any reason. Repeat this word or phrase to yourself over and over again. Stay with this one part of the text for a few minutes, even if it's only a single word. Resist judging or analyzing the word or phrase that has claimed your attention. Resist trying to make sense out of the choice, but instead, to receive it as a word God is giving you today from this reading.

After two or three minutes of silent reflection on your word or phrase, read the whole passage again, silently or aloud. Do so with this question as your guide: "How am I being called to respond to this word or phrase today?" Is there some invitation in the scripture for you, prompted through the word or phrase that has captured your attention? Something personal, something for someone you know, something you need to do in response, something for God? Do you feel called to change something or to stand firm in something in your life as a Christ-follower?

If you don't experience an invitation at this time, don't worry, but allow this scripture passage to go with you throughout the day. Remain open to how God might prompt an invitation and response at a later time. Spend at least five minutes reflecting on prayerful invitation from and response to the reading. When you feel you are ready to move on, offer a prayer to God for the possibilities of how this scripture may help shape your faithfulness.

Group Meeting Experience

1 Peter 2:4-10 | Chosen people

First Peter is written to people who wanted to go back to the loyalties that claimed their hearts and minds before encountering Christ. With this in mind, the writer wants them to reclaim their identity as covenant people. Using passages from the Old Testament with astounding literalism, Peter says to those who are tempted to go back to their old ways: You are the chosen people and heirs of God's faithful, promising love.

1. Here are some of the Old Testament passages that 1 Peter quotes in these verses: Psalms 34:8; 118:22; Isaiah 8:14-15; 28:16; 57:15; Hosea 2:23; and Exodus 19:6. Find these passages and read them aloud.

2. How do you understand the fact that 1 Peter can mix up these verses from all over and combine them into a kind of prophetic stew?

3. If Christians are now the chosen people, what do we understand about Jewish people? You might want to look briefly at Romans 9–11, where Paul wrestles with this question and insists that God is still, as always, the God of Jews as well as of Gentiles.

4. What about the role of God's destiny (or predestination) as implied in 1 Peter 2:8? Does this mean that our fates are determined by God from the beginning? If so, how do we understand our responsibility? If our decision to believe isn't determined by God, what does the passage suggest about those who don't trust God or behave responsibly with a changed life?

5. Look at 1 Peter 1:10-12. Does this passage help us see how our writer interprets the Old Testament?

SIGNS OF FAITHFUL LOVE

Whether God chooses us or we choose God, Covenant people lead changed lives that put faith into action.

Prophets: Isaiah 1–39 and the Book of the Twelve

DOING THE RIGHT THING
What should we do?

Bible Readings

Day 1: Isaiah 1; 5:1–7:17; 9:2-7; 11:1-10

Day 2: Hosea 1:1-9; 2; 11:1-9

Day 3: Amos 1:1–3:8; 5; 7:10-17

Day 4: Micah 1:1–3:12; 6:1-8

Day 5: Zephaniah 1; 3; Malachi 3–4

Day 6: Covenant Meditation on Micah 6:8

Day 7: Group Meeting Experience with Amos 5:7-24

Covenant Prayer

For those of us who are comfortable, whose songs drown out God's call in the cry of the needy

Let justice roll down like waters, and righteousness like an ever-flowing stream. (Amos 5:24)

For those of us who long for lasting harmony between the powerful and the weak

He has told you, human one, what is good and what the LORD requires. (Micah 6:8)

OUR LONGING FOR RELATIONSHIP

When we as God's children ignore our covenant with others and with the Lord, it breaks God's heart.

THE PROPHETS

A life-giving covenant is a relationship that expresses itself in love of neighbor, as well as in love of God.

John the Baptist addresses his audience like a prophet: "You children of snakes! Who warned you to escape from the angry judgment that is coming soon? Produce fruit that shows you have changed your hearts and lives. And don't even think about saying to yourselves, Abraham is our father" (Luke 3:7-8). Challenged, the crowd asks the question, "What then should we do?" (Luke 3:10), and John answers that doing the right thing is required. The right thing includes mutual care and sharing, responsible use of power in society, honesty, and respect for the less powerful.

John the Baptist, like the prophets who came before him, knew that the life-giving covenant that God establishes with God's people isn't a matter of pedigree or entitlement. It's a living relationship that expresses itself in love of neighbor, as well as in love of God. The prophets believed that to be truly religious was to live faithfully and justly. They especially held the wealthy and the powerful accountable, addressing most of their speeches to individuals with status and power and to those who lived in their rich and powerful cities. By their passion for justice, the prophets have become the great voice in the Bible—and in Western culture more broadly—for the ethical life.

John's judgment of his hearers' failures, like the judgments of the prophets before him, was harsh. The eighth-century BCE prophets we will study in this episode saw God's punishment for Israel's failures in the military invasions and widespread destruction of the Assyrian Empire's armies. We may have different opinions about the prophets' view that God is a God of judgment or that God uses one nation to punish another. But we can appreciate the prophets' passion for justice that drove these ideas of judgment. And we can also appreciate the persistent prophetic hope for renewal. Like the eighth-century prophets facing the destruction of Israel's and Judah's political life, and the loss of their religious centers to foreign invaders, John never closes the door of hope. "What then should we do?" is a hopeful and timely question today, as well.

ISAIAH OF JERUSALEM

The Prophets express God's passionate yearning to be our God.

Numerous men and women became prophets in ancient Israel, but we have available only some words from a few of them, preserved in collections and anthologies compiled and written after their proclamations were spoken. The Isaiah scroll is a compilation of the work of three prophets. Isaiah ben Amoz, active in Jerusalem during the second half of the eighth century BCE, concerns us in this episode (see Episode 21 for Isa 40–66). Isaiah 1–39, with the probable exception of chapters 24–27, contains his words. Unlike the other eighth-century prophets, Isaiah ben Amoz seems to have easy access to Judah's kings. His words are directed primarily to Jerusalem (known also as Zion) and to the Davidic monarchy, to which he appeals for justice. He sees the monarchy as the focus of divine displeasure, and he believes that the Davidic monarchy is central to the hope of restoration. God, after all, still offers a future for the covenant with David's house (2 Sam 7).

THE BOOK OF THE TWELVE

The "Book of the Twelve" is a single book (or scroll) in the Hebrew text of the Bible. It is the fourth book of the Latter Prophets (sometimes called Minor Prophets) following Isaiah, Jeremiah, and Ezekiel. The Christian canon counts the Latter Prophets as separate books. We will read selections from only five prophets, keeping them in canonical and historical order: Hosea, Amos, Micah, Zephaniah, and Malachi.

These prophets were different in time and place, in historical context, location in society, and of course, in personal interests and gifts. Hosea, Amos, and Micah share Isaiah's eighth-century context, while Zephaniah and Malachi are from later periods. It's possible, however, to see in all of them what Abraham Joshua Heschel long ago defined as the essence of prophecy in the Hebrew Bible: The prophets express the "pathos of God." The covenant that God established with Israel is a personal relationship in which both parties are affected by each other. The covenant isn't an impersonal contract. The prophets give expression to God's anger, aroused by social injustice even more than by willful disobedience about God's instructions. They also promise a coming judgment where accounts will be severely settled. At the same time, the "door of hope" (Hos 2:15) will ever be reopened, and restoration will always be possible, because God loves Israel as a parent loves a straying child, as a partner loves an errant spouse.

> **Optional:** *An additional video on defining a prophet is available for download from* **CovenantBibleStudy.com**.

Prophets in ancient Israel functioned as spokespeople for God and advocates for God's way in the world. Royal prophets had a place in the court and access to the king (Nathan in David's court, Isaiah to king Hezekiah). Others, like Amos and Hosea, came from humble or obscure settings. Together they bring messages of judgment on injustice and idolatry, and a promise that God's faithful love will reclaim a faithless people (such as in Hosea).

For a complete chart of the historical settings of the Prophetic Books, see the CEB Study Bible, *OT pages 1156–1157.*

Day 1: Isaiah 1; 5:1–7:17; 9:2-7; 11:1-10
Royal prophet

Isaiah begins with an accusation in the form of a dispute (Isa 1:2). Calling the heavens and the earth to witness was a traditional way of addressing the elders who settled family conflicts. The voice we hear—"I reared children; I raised them, and they turned against me!"—is that of a grieving parent. His stubborn children have refused to learn from punishment and continue to rebel, to the point that the community risks the fate of Sodom and Gomorrah (Gen 19:23-28). The grieving Lord rejects the sacrifices of the temple as "wickedness with celebration" (Isa 1:13) and insists that "Zion will be redeemed by justice, and those who change their lives by righteousness" (Isa 1:27). What angers God is clear: injustice and oppression of the weak and corruption at all levels of the clan and community.

There's a last offer by God. God is as unwilling to carry out the deserved destruction as God is anxious to keep open the possibility of change and deliverance. Isaiah 1:16-31 represents that offer, a call to "settle this" (Isa 1:18). Rather than trying to mend a broken relationship with God with religious rites, Jerusalem and its rulers have work to do throughout the community (Isa 1:16-17). Isaiah 1:21-23 makes it clear that God requires changes in the areas of public safety, financial integrity, consumer protection (watered-down beer?), honest government, and fair administration of justice, especially to the least powerful: the widows and the orphans. This, rather than more sacrifices, is what God requires, and in the rest of Isaiah 1 the threat of destruction turns into a promise of redemption.

The "song of the vineyard" in Isaiah 5:1-7 returns to the theme of God's disappointed expectations concerning Judah, still within the general framework of a family dispute. Here the prophet is using a bitter parody of a "love song," perhaps a song addressed to the bridegroom at a wedding. Such a song might have celebrated the expected crop of the vineyard (metaphorically, the children to come), but here the prophet turns it into condemnation of the people who have disappointed God (Isa 5:3, 7).

When foreign enemies threatened Judah and Jerusalem, Isaiah viewed their invasion as God's punishment, but he believed that God wouldn't allow his dearly loved city Jerusalem to fall into their hands. For Isaiah, that hope is rooted in God's covenant with David, in the survival of Jerusalem, and in the rule of a future righteous king of the house of David.

Isaiah 7 is spoken during an invasion of Judah by Israel's King Pekah and Syria's King Rezin (see 2 Kgs 16:1-9), who formed a coalition aimed at forcing Judah to join them in a revolt against Assyria. Isaiah tells Judah's King Ahaz that God would protect Jerusalem and preserve David's dynasty, and he confirms this with the sign of Immanuel (Isa 7:14-16). The "young woman" is probably a pregnant wife of Ahaz. By the time she gives birth, she will be able to give her newborn the joyous name "Immanuel" (God is with us) because the crisis posed by the attack of Israel and Syria will be over.

This narrative and other speeches in Isaiah—for example, the lovely prediction of an ideal future Davidic ruler leading to the establishment of a peaceable kingdom found in Isaiah 11:1-9—helped to shape later Jewish and Christian ideas of a messiah, a future descendant of David who would renew God's ancient promises. As we read these passages, remember that the qualities of the ideal king (Isa 11:2-5) represent precisely the values that covenant people are to establish in their social, economic, and political lives. The peaceful and lasting harmony between the powerful and the weak, which Isaiah 11:6-9 so beautifully evokes, is indeed God's will for covenant people everywhere.

Can you think of a time when you felt that God was angry with you or your family or your community? Did that sense of anger give way to forgiveness and hope?

Day 2: Hosea 1:1-9; 2; 11:1-9
How can I give you up, Ephraim?

Hosea's prophetic activity took place in the northern kingdom of Israel (Ephraim) in the years before its capital, Samaria, fell to the Assyrians (721 BCE), beginning in the reign of Jeroboam (Hos 1:1). He was a contemporary of Isaiah, who prophesied to the southern kingdom of Judah and to its capital, Jerusalem.

Hosea chooses images from the sphere of family life and human love (husband and wife; parent and child) to express God's relationship with God's dearly loved people, even if they are less than faithful. Canaanite shrines were devoted to the Canaanite god Baal (whose name means "lord," "owner," "husband"). These worship centers tried to secure fertility for families and crops, and they were popular in Israel and Judah in the eighth century BCE. Hosea condemns the worship of Baal, mingled and confused with the worship of Yahweh (Hos 2:8, 16-17), calling it adultery, promiscuity, or prostitution. To dramatize God's relationship to a faithless Israel, Hosea marries a prostitute (Hos 1:2). Hosea's marriage to Gomer produced three children, whose names symbolize Israel's rejection of its covenant relationship to God: Jezreel (named after the site of Jehu's massacre of members of the previous ruling house in 2 Kgs 9:14–10:11), "No Compassion," and "Not My People." The name of the last child reverses the formula used in Exodus 6:7 and Leviticus 26:12 to signal the establishment of the covenant.

In Hosea 2:2 we find the covenant metaphor extending to marriage and divorce: "She is not my wife, and I am not her husband." Hosea's address to his children in Hosea 2 is also clearly God addressing Israel, and the grief of God over Israel's idolatry shows through the grief of the prophet over Gomer's adultery. Hosea 2:8 poignantly asserts that going after Baal was fruitless, since all along it was Yahweh who "gave her the corn, the new wine, and the fresh oil, and . . . much silver, and gold that they used for Baal." From Hosea 2:14 on, the marriage is renewed (note the reference to the exodus as a honeymoon in Hos 2:15), and Yahweh promises a new covenant that will involve all nature and ensure universal peace. The lovely poetic reversal of the divorce ends with the renewal of the relationship: "You are my people . . . You are my God" (Hos 2:19-23).

In Hosea 11:1-9, the prophet turns to the image of a parent with an errant grown child, who finds that the tender feelings their relationship once evoked are still there: "When Israel was a child, I loved him, and out of Egypt I called my son." Hosea 11:3-4 is heart-rending, and Hosea dares to tell us that it's God's heart that is torn apart. Ephraim (Israel) will suffer, inevitably—but his grieving parent can't bear to give him up (Hos 11:8). In a situation that would destroy a human parent, however, God can decide against anger and the inevitability of Ephraim's destruction (Hos 11:9).

At times, most people will feel estranged or distant from God. If this happens, recall such a time and try to express how God's heart was affected. If it helps, imagine how a parent feels when a child isn't relating or communicating.

Day 3: Amos 1:1–3:8; 5; 7:10-17
A lion has roared.

Amos lived in Tekoa, a village on the edge of the desert near Bethlehem in the southern kingdom of Judah. He wasn't a "professional" prophet but "a shepherd, and a trimmer of sycamore trees" (Amos 7:14). It's unusual that Amos, a southerner, prophesied in Bethel, the royal sanctuary of the northern kingdom. The editorial note in Amos 1:1 places the prophet's words at "two years before the earthquake," a reference to a major earthquake dated by archaeology to 760 BCE. He, too, was an eighth-century contemporary of Isaiah and Hosea.

> **Optional:** *An additional video on Isaiah and Amos is available for download from* **CovenantBibleStudy.com**.

Amos' words about the Lord roaring like a lion in Amos 1:2 and in Amos 3:8 frame six speeches of doom to foreign nations (Amos 1:3–2:3), one to Judah (Amos 2:4-5), and a climactic one addressed to Israel (Amos 2:6-16). The crimes of the six foreign nations—Damascus/Syria, the Philistines (Gaza, Ashdod, Ekron, and Ashkelon), Tyre/the Phoenicians, Edom, Ammon, and Moab—are all war crimes: committing atrocities, selling the defeated into slavery, or betraying treaty obligations. In each case, God will inflict punishment through war, sending fire to destroy fortifications, breaking down gates, defeating armies, and deporting rulers.

Judah's crime is different: "because they have rejected the Instruction (Torah) of the LORD, and haven't kept his laws" (Amos 2:4). They have rejected their covenant responsibilities. The crime of Israel (Amos 2:6-12) is an amplification of Judah's crime. Amos criticizes corruption of justice to the detriment of the innocent poor, oppression of the powerless by the powerful, sexual abuse, worship celebrations financed by illegal gains extorted from the poor, refusal to respect the solemn pledge of nazirites, and failure to listen to the prophets. The most powerful expression of Amos' conviction that the covenant relationship between God and Israel can carry terrible consequences comes in Amos 3:1-2, which is directed against "the whole family that I brought out of the land of Egypt": "You only have I loved so deeply of all the families of the earth. Therefore, I will punish you for all your wrongdoing." That "therefore" bears the weight of the grief and disappointment God feels at the people's betrayal of God's love, and the pain of having to punish their wrongdoing.

What types of behavior in our present-day society would you want God to punish?

Day 4: Micah 1:1–3:12; 6:1-8
What the Lord requires from you

Micah came from Moresheth, a village in the southern kingdom of Judah, which, if it is the village mentioned by the prophet in Micah 1:14, may have been located near the Philistine city of Gath. Micah was an eighth-century contemporary of Isaiah, Hosea, and Amos. Nearly a century later, defenders of Jeremiah, accused of treason for speaking against the king, successfully cited in his defense "Micah of Moresheth, who prophesied during the rule of [King] Hezekiah" (Jer 26:18).

Micah 1:2–3:12 tells of the terrifying destruction that the Lord is already bringing upon the land by the Assyrian invasion of 701 BCE, when many of the towns of Judah were taken. Micah places the blame for the Assyrian invasion on the two capitals, Samaria and Jerusalem (Mic 1:5). He focuses on the guilt of land-grabbing speculators and of political and religious leaders who forbid the prophet from condemning them while they evict women and children from their homes (Mic 2:1-11). Micah sarcastically says that they would rather listen to a false prophet who would preach to them for wine and beer. The sarcasm turns gruesome in the image that opens Micah 3, where the rulers of the northern kingdom of Israel who are in charge of administering justice "devour the flesh of my people" (Mic 3:3). In the southern kingdom, fraudulent prophets, corrupt judges, and venal priests have joined with the rulers "who build Zion with bloodshed and Jerusalem with injustice" (Mic 3:10). The consequence is inevitable: "Zion will be plowed like a field" (Mic 3:12).

Micah 6:1-8 brings back the image of the Lord's dispute with God's people, which includes a recital of God's "righteous acts" in the history of Israel, beginning with the exodus (Mic 6:4). What does the Lord require? Micah answers his own question, first by ridiculing the value of offerings and sacrifices with mounting exaggeration (Mic 6:6-7), and then by stating what fidelity to the covenant really requires in the brilliant words of verse 8: "to do justice, embrace faithful love, and walk humbly with your God."

Can you think of a contemporary example of a person who pursued justice, embraced faithful love, and walked humbly with God? Try to think of someone you know.

Day 5: Zephaniah 1; 3; Malachi 3–4
The great day of the Lord is near.

Zephaniah's editor—whoever compiled Zephaniah in its final form—places him a century later than the prophets above. This makes Zephaniah a contemporary of Jeremiah, who also prophesied during the reign of Josiah (640–609 BCE), Judah's king when the great Babylonian Empire was on the rise. His editor gives him an unusually long genealogy, going back to his great-great-grandfather Hezekiah (Zeph 1:1). There is no evidence that this was the eighth-century King Hezekiah under whom Isaiah prophesied, nor that Hezekiah had a son named Amariah, but some have claimed that Zephaniah was of David's line.

For Zephaniah, "the day of the LORD" (Zeph 1:7) is a day yet to come, but near, in which the Lord will appear to wage victorious battle against God's enemies, and to rule, judge, and heal the earth. As we have seen, not only the foreign nations will come under judgment, but the people of God also risk falling into the same category. Destruction and judgment on Judah and Jerusalem are overwhelming in Zephaniah's speeches, but he sees them as the awful consequences of a covenant failure full of unethical conduct: violence and deceit, corrupt business practices, irresponsible wealth, cruel government, and unfair courts (Zeph 1:9-13; 3:1-3). At the same time, references to the "day of the LORD," even those that promise a thorough destruction of humankind as Zephaniah 1 does, are followed by promises of a few survivors (Zeph 3:9-20) and revival of a faithful people.

Malachi means "my messenger." It is a work written after the exile and addressed to the Jerusalem priesthood sometime during the latter half of the fifth century BCE. This was the period of reconstruction after the fall of Jerusalem (586 BCE) and the Babylonian exile (586–539 BCE).

Like the prophets before him, Malachi calls his contemporaries to covenant faithfulness, reminding them about the life of justice that the covenant relationship requires. In Malachi 3:1, the "messenger of the covenant"—identified as Elijah in Malachi 4:5—is announced, coming before the final judgment to purify the temple and the Levites, to rid society of all who offend against justice, and to call for a return to the LORD, who says: "Return to me and I will return to you" (Mal 3:7).

Do you think we live in a just society, like the world required by the Old Testament prophets?

Day 6: Micah 6:8

Covenant Meditation: Justice, love, and humility

Embedded deeply in the conscience and memory of God's people is a very brief text that states what fidelity to the covenant really requires. These words glisten in Micah 6:8: "He has told you, human one, what is good and what the LORD requires from you: to do justice, embrace faithful love, and walk humbly with your God."

Few scriptures better capture the essence of the human side of our life-giving covenant with God—a covenant into which God invites us. It is a relationship that God establishes with us, not the other way around.

So for our spiritual reading practice this week, we will use this text to form a prayer that we can take with us wherever we go. You may want to rephrase the text into a prayer you can remember by heart, creating a personal prayer such as: "Lord, help me to do justice, embrace love, and walk humbly" or simply, "Teach me to be just, loving, and humble, God." Or you may find that memorizing the text just as it is will strengthen this experience of praying the scripture. Either way, these powerful words from Micah are forever ours to help guide us in the covenant life with God.

Once you have created or memorized your prayer, take some time (at least a few minutes) to repeat the prayer in silence or aloud. As this day and week move forward, recall your prayer with intention, perhaps associating it with an activity that occurs often throughout the day, such as waiting at a yellow light, washing your hands, or sitting down to read your e-mail. In this way, you can begin to develop a more frequent practice of praying the scripture by connecting it to a habit you've already formed.

Group Meeting Experience

Amos 5:7-24 | Seek good.

Of all the prophets, Amos, the earliest writing prophet, was probably the harshest critic of his people's injustices. As is typical of prophetic speeches, this one alternates between criticism of the people's failures and prediction of the consequences of these failures. Amos' aim isn't to consign his people to destruction, but to encourage them to live faithfully (Amos 5:14-15, 24).

1. Outline Amos' speech by identifying which sections critique the people's behavior and which sections describe the consequences of the people's behavior. From the sections of Amos' speech that you've identified as criticizing the people's behavior, list the specific crimes that Amos emphasizes. What would you describe as the modern equivalents of the specific crimes Amos emphasizes?

2. Amos believed the consequences of unfaithful behavior to be the punishment of God delivered by the invading Assyrian armies. How do the images of punishment in this speech reflect such an invasion?

3. If Amos saw God's punishment for injustice in terms of a defeat in war, how do you see the consequences of faithless behavior today? How do we experience the consequences of disregarding covenant responsibility and of not doing the right thing?

4. Amos says, "Seek good and not evil, that you may live" (Amos 5:14). Given his specific criticisms of his people's failures in this speech, what do you think seeking good—doing the right thing—meant for him? What does it mean for you?

5. Dr. Martin Luther King, Jr., often quoted Amos 5:24 in his sermons calling for equality in American society. Whom would you identify as prophetic figures today?

SIGNS OF FAITHFUL LOVE

Covenant people practice mutual care and sharing, responsible use of power in society, honesty, and respect for the less powerful.

Well done!

You have completed the second participant guide, *Living the Covenant*. You studied daily from scripture about the importance of living out your covenant with God and others. In your Covenant group, you saw signs of faithful love and life that are always present among God's friends. Your relationships are deepening.

By now you have also developed a habit for reading the Bible daily. The stress of daily life can't outweigh the spiritual benefits of sharing your hopes, divine promises, and personal yearnings with your Covenant group.

Keep going! You are two-thirds of the way there. You can do it. The Bible is a big, ancient collection of books, and getting the "big picture" for the whole Bible is already helping you grow and become more faithful as a friend, parent, coworker, or leader. The loyal relationships cultivated in your Covenant group will produce fruit for the rest of your life.

Whether your group takes a break or continues right away, *Trusting the Covenant* is waiting for your input. You now understand how the biblical God relates to us through covenant and how we live out our faith in a community of friends who love God. In the third and last participant guide, you will learn how faithful and even faithless people somehow find a way to trust God in the face of overwhelming disappointment and devastating setbacks.